Pandas *to* Penguins

W. L. MOODY JR.
NATURAL HISTORY
SERIES

Texas A&M
University Press
College Station

Pandas *to* Penguins

ETHICAL ENCOUNTERS WITH ANIMALS AT RISK

Melissa
Gaskill

This paper meets the requirements
of ANSI/NISO Z39.48–1992 (Permanence of Paper).
Binding materials have been chosen for durability.
Manufactured in China by Everbest Printing Co.
through FCI Print Group

Library of Congress Cataloging-in-Publication Data

Names: Gaskill, Melissa, author.
Title: Pandas to penguins : ethical encounters with animals at risk /
   Melissa Gaskill.
Other titles: W.L. Moody Jr. natural history series ; no. 29.
Description: First edition. | College Station : Texas A&M University Press,
   [2018] | Series: W.L. Moody Jr. natural history series ; number
   twenty-nine | Includes index.
Identifiers: LCCN 2018013999 | ISBN 9781623496692 (book/flexbound (with
   flaps) : alk. paper)
Subjects: LCSH: Wildlife watching--Moral and ethical aspects. |
   Wildlife-related recreation industry--Moral and ethical aspects. |
   Ecotourism. | Endangered species.
Classification: LCC QL60 .G37 2018 | DDC 598.47--dc23 LC record available at
https://lccn.loc.gov/2018013999
Display art by Yoko Design / Shutterstock

Contents

Preface

The condition of wildlife and habitats around the world changes at an ever-increasing pace. In October 2016, the World Wildlife Fund's "Living Planet Index" stated that global populations of fish, birds, mammals, amphibians, and reptiles declined by 58 percent between 1970 and 2012. If current trends continue, the report predicts that decline could reach two-thirds by 2020. According to the National Wildlife Federation, more than 8,000 species in the United States alone face uncertain futures.

The animals featured in this book remain in sufficient numbers, at least in isolated areas, to offer at least a chance of seeing them on the trips covered here. That can all change, though, from the time of this writing or in the months following publication of this book. In fact, my original list of animals included black rhinos, but after speaking with several experts and tour guides, I decided that, before this book reached readers' hands, black rhino numbers would fall so low that seeing them would be nearly impossible—or they may even become extinct. Some of the animals included here teeter on the brink and could become harder and harder to see, or disappear entirely.

Governments, economic situations, and local situations also change. While the information provided is as accurate as possible, it may not remain so over time. Changes in local conditions, continued destruction of habitat, decay of infrastructure, or political turmoil all can quickly reduce animal populations. These factors also may necessitate changes to itineraries or make it no longer possible to visit certain destinations. Responsible tour outfitters do their best to keep up with situations in the places to which they travel and continue to support wildlife and wild places through tourism whenever possible. If you travel on your own, consult with these companies as well as other resources for information about current conditions.

Extinction is tragic but not inevitable. We can all do something to make a difference. I encourage you to support responsible tourism that helps animals at risk.

Acknowledgments

The author thanks staff and scientists at the US Fish and Wildlife Service, National Oceanic and Atmospheric Administration, and International Union for the Conservation of Nature for their input. This book drew on information about specific species and threats to their survival and conservation efforts from the World Wildlife Fund, ARKive, the National Wildlife Federation, Defenders of Wildlife, the Center for Biodiversity, National Geographic, Natural Resources Defense Council, and Earthjustice. See the Wild provided invaluable guidance on sustainable tourism practices and choosing responsible outfitters.

Pandas *to* Penguins

Animals at Risk
and Responsible Wildlife Tourism

For centuries, we humans have lived ever more separate from nature. Yet the natural world remains an integral part of us, in ways we may not notice yet cannot resist. The wonder of a dark night sky sprinkled with tiny diamonds of light brings us to a halt, necks craned, mouths open. Waves rolling onto the beach lure us to the shore, where we sit, mesmerized by their power and rhythm, or we find ourselves pulled into the water to let them percuss against us. The thick quiet of deep woods brings stillness to our frantic minds; a palette of wildflowers painting a hillside slows our heartbeats.

Perhaps nothing about nature calls to us as deeply as wild animals. To see an enormous whale leaping out of the water, the eerily human eyes of a gorilla, or the comical waddle of a penguin; to hear the ethereal howl of a wolf or majestic roar of a lion—these experiences change us. Somehow, deep down, we know we share our planet, our ancestry, and our fate with these creatures, that at some level each represents our kin.

Many wild animals possess stunning beauty—a richly spotted jaguar, brightly colored macaw, furry fox, or delicately patterned monarch butterfly. We capture this beauty in photographs so we can return to it again and again.

Others we find more entertaining than beautiful. We smile at the ungainliness of a seal on land, the playfulness of a leaping dolphin, or funny face of a panda bear. Some simply fascinate us, with bizarre rituals, mysterious lives, or impressive size and strength.

People find wildlife so appealing that millions of us plan entire vacations around the chance to see creatures in their native surroundings or go out of our way to incorporate wildlife experiences into our outings. At home, we put up bird feeders in our yards, toss crumbs to squirrels, and buy calendars and coffee table books with beautiful images of wildlife.

It turns out that, according to a large and growing body of research, we *need* connections to nature. Interacting with it boosts our immune systems, protects against a wide range of diseases and disorders, and generally makes us healthier and happier—improving sleep and memory, enhancing creativity and critical thinking skills, and lowering stress levels and blood pressure.

Wildlife Tourism

Given all that, it comes as no surprise that visits to wildlife-related tourist attractions may account for as much as 20 to 40 percent of the worldwide tourism industry. According to a study funded by World Animal Protection published in late 2015, tourism accounts for 9 percent of global gross domestic product (GDP) and in 2013 had a worth of more than one trillion US dollars. It represents 1.1 billion tourist arrivals a year and provides 1 in 11 jobs worldwide.*

For that study, the researchers divided wildlife tourism into four broad categories: wildlife watching, meaning viewing or otherwise interacting with free-ranging animals; captive-wildlife tourism, or viewing animals in confinement such as zoos, wildlife parks, animal sanctuaries, and aquaria; hunting; and fishing. Hunting and fishing are consumptive activities, of course, with the animal or fish removed from the environment (in most cases). Captive-wildlife tourism also removes animals from the wild, albeit alive, often taking them great distances and into vastly different conditions.

The study found that many of these activities actually harm the wel-

* See Tom P. Moorhouse, Cecilia A. L. Dahlsjö, Sandra E. Baker, Neil C. D'Cruze, and David W. Macdonald, "The Customer Isn't Always Right—Conservation and Animal Welfare Implications of the Increasing Demand for Wildlife Tourism," *PLOS One*, October 21, 2015, http://journals.plos.org/plosone/article?id=10.1371/journal.pone.0138939.

fare of animals. Problems generally trace to removing wildlife from the wild for the pleasure of humans. Some examples:

- A minimum of 22,218 great apes were lost from the wild through illegal activity from 2005 to 2011, according to the United Nations Environmental Programme's Great Apes Survival Partnership (http://www.un-grasp.org/stolen-apes-report/).

- Dolphins and whales captured in the wild end up in various facilities, separated from their highly functioning social units and often without adequate space or stimulation. Japan's infamous Taiji dolphin hunt in 2015 sold 117 dolphins to unaccredited aquariums or directly to wildlife dealers (http://www.japantimes .co.jp/news/2016/05/12 /national/despite-jaza-acquisition-ban -sales-taiji-drive-hunt -dolphins-40/#.V1iRhb71IX7). (http://www .cetabase.org/) tracks dolphins and whales at hundreds of facilities around the world.

- Facilities where tourists can pet lion cubs or walk with tame lions often sell adult animals for "canned hunts" where shooters kill them under controlled conditions, says Luke Hunter, chief conservation officer at Panthera, a global wild cat conservation organization (https://www.panthera.org). Research has shown that captive-bred lions released into the wild seldom survive. Further, these businesses divert funds from legitimate conservation activities and deceive well-meaning tourists into believing they are helping the species when they are not.

- A tiger temple in Thailand, Wat Pa Luangta Bua Yannasampanno, charged tourists to pose for photos with tigers and feed cubs and claimed to be an animal sanctuary but turned out to be a front for trafficking in tiger parts. Monks bred the animals for profit. Officials with the Department of National Parks found more than 70 dead tiger cubs in freezers and jars at the temple and shut down the facility. Tiger parts are used in traditional Chinese medicine, which attributes many benefits to tiger bone. Any benefits come from the calcium content of the bone, however, which means other sources of calcium would be just as effective (http://news.mongabay.com/2010/06 /tiger-farming-and-traditional-chinese-medicine/).

Animals kept in captivity experience a diminished quality of life. Travelers who seek an authentic experience observing free and wild animals are likely to find captive experiences disappointing. Seeing an orca in a small tank or a lion in a cage pales in comparison to watching a wild whale leap from the open ocean or a pride of lions resting regally on the savanna.

Tourism can have negative effects on animals in the wild as well. In national parks in Africa and India, for example, tour jeeps have been seen harassing or chasing animals, the guides doing their best to give paying clients what they see as a better experience by getting them closer (often encouraged by thrill-seeking clients). The same thing can happen with whale- and dolphin-watching tours, with boats chasing the animals and motoring in too close to groups that may be feeding or caring for young. Pursuit and close contact can stress animals and even endanger visitors.

Fortunately, wildlife-watching tourism done right—bringing people into encounters with animals living in the wild while minimizing interference with those animals as much as possible—can benefit both people and animals. It generates jobs and millions of dollars for local communities, which in turn tends to encourage those communities to conserve wildlife and wildlife habitats. It offers opportunities to educate tourists, which can promote positive attitudes toward species preservation and conservation in general.

Around the world, wildlife tourism already involves large numbers of animals and tourists, and experts predict significant increases in global tourism. For wildlife tourism to do more good than harm, travelers need to understand the effects of their choices and need guidance in making those choices.

This book, more than a kind of wildlife bucket list or an exhortation to "see them before they're gone," is intended to identify wildlife experiences that can be life changing for people as well as animals. When you sign up for a trip with a responsible, sustainably operated outfitter, you give something back. Your support can help protect and conserve animals both for their own intrinsic value and for others to have the same amazing experience you did.

Choosing a Responsible Operator

Traveling with a responsible tour operator can be the best way to travel to remote and sensitive areas. The operators featured in this book have established relationships with local entities, obtain any required permits, and follow rules and regulations concerning travel within protected areas. They also follow these four important criteria for responsible wildlife tourism:

1. They provide direct support for wildlife conservation through monetary and in-kind donations or volunteer support (or both).

2. They include a strong educational element, informing travelers about the specific animals and the environment in which the animals live, as well as the local community, and how the two interact.

3. They minimize their environmental impact as much as possible, actively reducing waste, greenhouse gas pollution, and other negative effects of their activities.

4. They patronize local businesses, employing local guides and locally owned services such as transportation, accommodations, and restaurants wherever possible. This practice provides income directly to people living in these areas, creating economic opportunity and empowering communities. This support of local busi-

nesses and people is more equitable and sustainable in the long term than programs that make monetary or in-kind donations on a one-time or sporadic basis.

In addition, responsible operators follow good wildlife-watching practices on their trips, such as the following:

- Never feed wild animals.
- Keep a respectable distance.
- Avoid chasing or following wildlife.
- Avoid touching animals.
- Limit watching times to avoid stressing animals.

Travelers should patronize captive wildlife facilities only if they are actively involved in appropriate reintroduction to the wild or care for animals unable to return to the wild.

Before you book a trip or tour, ask questions about the company's policies. Any reputable company will provide this information gladly—if it acts responsibly, it wants you to know. Consider lack of knowledge or evasiveness a red flag.

Tour operators featured in this book have well-established reputations and long track records traveling to the particular place or places for which they are recommended. They were chosen by the author and did not give or receive anything in return.

Photographing Wildlife Responsibly

Many people travel to see wildlife to take photographs. In addition to practicing responsible viewing of wildlife, it is important to follow responsible practices for taking pictures. The welfare of the animal always ranks above a person's desire to obtain a photograph. In general, that means avoiding any action that might interfere with natural wildlife behavior or habituate wild animals to humans. Specifically, keep these guidelines in mind:

- Keep an appropriate distance. If the animal stops what it is doing—resting or feeding, for example—you are too close. If it moves, you definitely crossed the line. The quality of current telephoto technology makes getting physically close unnecessary at any rate.

- Take care to never position yourself between a parent and its offspring. This can cause serious distress for the young and the mother and can be dangerous for you.

- Never follow or corner an animal or make noises to distract or startle it. This can cause the animal stress or cause it to waste valuable energy getting away from you, and the effect is cumulative—you may be the tenth or hundredth person to disturb the animal that day.

- Never feed wildlife or leave food out to attract animals. This results in habituation, which increases human/wildlife conflict and can lead to an animal being killed. It also can result in disease or injury for either party.

- Consider occasionally putting your camera away and simply focusing on the experience. When wildlife-watching outings turn into semi-circuses, with everyone jostling for position and caring only about getting the right shot, it becomes less enjoyable for everyone—including, most likely, the animals. Observe, appreciate, savor—and then, remember.

Animals in This Guide

This guide presents 26 specific wild animals. Each met three basic criteria: the species faces some level of risk to its survival, it has reasonably accessible habitat where travelers can view the animal in its natural setting in the wild, and the animal or habitat benefits directly from responsible tourism.

What Does At-Risk Mean?

The animals in this guide (1) either appear on the International Union for the Conservation of Nature Red List or the United States Endangered Species list, or both; (2) have been identified as in trouble by some other agency; or (3) face imminent threats such as loss of habitat but, for various reasons, do not yet have an official endangered status. Each section gives details on the particular animal's status and why it appears in this book.

Union for the Conservation of Nature (IUCN) Red List

The IUCN includes more than 1,300 member organizations and the resources of some 16,000 experts, serving as the "global authority on the status of the natural world and the measures needed to safeguard it" (www.iucnredlist.org/). For more than 50 years, the IUCN Global Species Programme has assessed the status of species around the globe, using objective, scientifically based information to identify those threatened with extinction so that they may be conserved. Its IUCN Red List of Threatened Species provides taxonomic, conservation status, and distribution information on plants, fungi, and animals, ranking them from Least Concern to Extinct. Species listed as Critically Endangered, Endangered, and Vulnerable face the highest risk of extinction. The program currently manages data on more than 79,000 species, with approximately 64,000 of those well documented. This represents a very small number of the world's plant, fungi, and animal species; the organization has a target of 160,000 species by 2020 in its strategic plan.

Partners working on the Red List include BirdLife International, Botanical Gardens Conservation International, Conservation International, Microsoft, NatureServe, Royal Botanic Gardens Kew, Texas A&M University, the Institute of Zoology at the Zoological Society of London, Sapienza University of Rome, and WildScreen.

The IUCN Red List graciously provided permission to use information in this book about listed species from its extensive database.

Convention on International Trade in Endangered Species of Wild Fauna and Flora (CITES)

CITES, an international agreement between governments, aims to "ensure that international trade in specimens of wild animals and plants does not threaten their survival" (https://cites.org/eng). International wildlife trade represents billions of dollars annually and involves hundreds of millions of plant and animal specimens. This trade ranges from live animals to products made from them, including leather and fur goods, decorative items, and supposedly medicinal compounds made from animal parts. Such trade has heavily depleted the populations of some animal species, such as tigers and elephants.

Much of this trade crosses international borders, so efforts to control it require international cooperation. CITES provides a vehicle for that cooperation, contributing to the protection of more than 35,000 species of animals and plants. Countries agreeing to the convention or those that joined CITES are known as parties. CITES is legally binding on parties but does not take the place of national laws. Domestic legislation adopted in each individual country ensures implementation of CITES.

Parties must administer a system for licensing import and export of covered species, which are listed in three appendices, based on the degree of protection needed. Appendix I includes species threatened with extinction and permits trade in their specimens only in exceptional circumstances. As of summer 2016, it included 931 species and 47 subspecies. Appendix II includes species not necessarily threatened with extinction but that could become so without control of trade involving them. It includes 34,419 species and 11 subspecies. Appendix III contains species that at least one country protects and that has asked for assistance from other parties in controlling the trade. It includes 147 species and 13 subspecies.

US Endangered Species Act (ESA)

The ESA was passed in 1973 to "conserve endangered and threatened species and the ecosystems on which they depend as key components of America's heritage," according to the Interior Department's US Fish and Wildlife Service (FWS; https://www.fws.gov/endangered/). It stands as one of this country's most successful environmental laws in terms of accomplishing its intent—protecting biodiversity in the United States and around the world and preventing extinction of at-risk plants and animals. It has also achieved full recovery, followed by removal from the endangered list, for many species.

Less than 1 percent of species granted protection under the ESA have subsequently gone extinct, and the longer a species remains listed, the more likely its recovery. Those species for which the act has been used to designate critical habitat have twice as much chance of recovering as those that lack such a designation. A listing of Endangered means a species faces danger of extinction throughout all or a significant portion of its range. A listing of Threatened means a species is likely to become endangered within the foreseeable future.

According to the act, a species is added to the list based on these factors:

- The present or threatened destruction, modification, or curtailment of its habitat or range
- Overutilization for commercial, recreational, scientific, or educational purposes
- Disease or predation
- The inadequacy of existing regulatory mechanisms
- Other natural or human-made factors affecting its survival

Co-administered by FWS and the Commerce Department's National Marine Fisheries Service, the ESA currently protects roughly 1,436 US species and 618 foreign species. As of summer 2016, 103 mammal, 98 bird, 46 reptile, 35 amphibian, and 163 fish species were on the list as Endangered or Threatened. This does not include invertebrate animals (clams, snails, insects, arachnids, crustaceans, and corals), plants, or foreign species.

In addition, 59 species were candidates for listing, meaning that FWS biologists have assessed their status as meeting the definition of Threatened or Endangered and published public notice of this assessment. At this point, the species warrants listing, but higher priorities preclude that action. Given the number of candidate species and the time line of a listing decision, the agency assigns a priority reflecting the degree or magnitude of threats to a species' survival. Candidates are reviewed annually, and successful conservation efforts may warrant removing a species from the candidate list. Any member of the public can petition the agency to consider a species for listing, but these requests need supporting biological data. Find more details about the listing process on the FWS website: https://www.fws.gov/endangered/esa-library /pdf/listing.pdf.

The law provides protection for listed species, including protection from adverse effects of federal activities and restrictions on its take, transport, or sale. "Take" means "to harass, harm, pursue, hunt, shoot, wound, kill, trap, capture, or collect or attempt to engage in any such conduct." In this definition, "harm" means an act that kills or injures wildlife, which can include significant modification or degradation of habitat that significantly impairs essential behaviors such as breeding, feeding, or sheltering. (Read more about this online at https://www.fws .gov/endangered/esa-library/pdf/ESA_basics.pdf.)

Listing also gives the FWS authority to develop and carry out recovery plans and purchase important habitat, and the law provides cooperating state and commonwealth wildlife agencies with federal aid. To date, 63 species have been delisted or removed from the list, most because of reclassification as recovered or no longer needing protection, but some due to extinction.

The FWS also can designate critical habitat for a species. The ESA defines critical habitat as "geographic areas containing features essential to the conservation of a threatened or endangered species and that may require special management considerations or protection." Designation does not affect landownership and does not stop private landowners from taking actions on their own land, as long as those activities do not require federal funding or permits.

ESA Success Stories

"The ESA is a safety net for wildlife, plants, and fish on the brink of extinction," says Rebecca Riley, senior attorney for the Natural Resources Defense Council. "Really one of our most successful laws, it has helped hundreds of species recover from that brink." However, not everyone loves the ESA. Some business interests claim it thwarts economic opportunities, extractive industries such as oil and gas often find its requirements onerous, and landowners in some areas chafe at restrictions it places on their ability to use their property as they see fit.

Some opponents say that the ESA should take into account the potential economic impacts of protection for a species. However, the ESA expressly requires that listing decisions be based solely on the best available science. Melinda Taylor, senior lecturer and executive director of the University of Texas School of Law's Center for Global Energy, International Arbitration, and Environmental Law, explains that Congress intentionally avoided making economics part of listing decisions, believing that deciding whether or not a species is endangered should be based solely on what science says about its status and risk of extinction. For a listed species, however, economics does play a role in decisions about how to best help it recover. In addition, determining boundaries of critical habitat requires consideration of economic and other effects.

The choice is not either endangered species or a healthy economy. "We have been successfully using the ESA for decades now, and what we've seen is that protection of species and their habitat absolutely can coexist with a healthy economy," Riley says. "In fact, in many cases, promoting the health of species and their ecosystems can contribute to a healthy economy."

The healthy ecosystems that result from conserving habitat and wild animals and plants provide benefits worth billions of dollars, including medicines, erosion control, cleaner air and water, soil maintenance, flood control, and abundant natural resources. According to Defenders of Wildlife, wildlife-related tourism pumps additional billions of dollars into our local and national economies. Furthermore, the ESA is a very flexible environmental law, providing many exceptions and alternatives that allow economic growth. In practice, it has permanently stopped very few development projects in its history. In general, Taylor adds, Americans care about endangered species and repeatedly rebuff attempts to weaken the act.

A study by the Center for Biological Diversity (CBD) of all endangered species in the northeastern United States found 93 percent of them increased in number or remained stable since being placed on the Endangered list. Birds represent one of the ESA's most spectacular successes; CBD reported in 2016 that 85 percent of listed continental US bird species increased in population or stabilized after receiving protection. Birds not protected under the ESA have declined on average 24 percent since 1974. Success stories include the iconic bald eagle, which increased from 416 pairs in 1963 to 9,789 pairs in 2006; peregrine falcons, which increased from 324 to 1,700 pairs between 1975 and 2000; the gray whale, which increased from 13,095 in 1968 to 26,635 individuals in 1998; and the grizzly bear, which increased from 224 to more than 700 bears in the Yellowstone area between 1975 and 2016.

As FWS states on its website, the ESA has "helped stabilize populations of species at risk, prevent the extinction of many others, and conserve the habitats upon which they depend. All Americans can take pride in the fact that, under the ESA, California condor, grizzly bear, Okaloosa darter, whooping crane, and black-footed ferret have all been brought back from the brink of extinction. We can also celebrate that many other species no longer need the ESA's protection and have been re-moved from the list of endangered and threatened species, including the bald eagle—the very symbol of our nation's strength."

The ESA works, Riley notes, but lack of congressional funding threat-ens that success. "For years, Congress has failed to allocate sufficient resources to protect endangered species, and, as a result, those species have suffered. It doesn't make sense to list a species only to see it dwin-dle due to lack of protection." The goal of a listing is to bring a species back, and the best outcome is taking it off the list because it has re-covered. Opposition to listings creates another problem. "Until a spe-cies is on the list, it doesn't get the resources it needs to recover," she adds. "The thing to know about recovery is that it is not a quick process. We can't expect species to recover overnight; some have faced serious threats for decades if not centuries, and those threats don't magically disappear when we put a species on the list. But with time, resources and effort we can bring species back. We have."

Marine Mammal Protection Act (MMPA)

In the United States, the MMPA, enacted in 1972, protects all marine mammals (www.nmfs.noaa.gov/pr/laws/mmpa/). This law "prohibits, with certain exceptions, the take of marine mammals in US waters and by US citizens on the high seas, and importation of marine mammals and marine mammal products into the US." Exceptions include small takes incidental to certain activities, including commercial fishing and scientific research. The act recognized that, as a result of human activi-ties, some marine mammal species or stocks faced extinction or deple-tion and that their populations must not be depleted or permitted to fall below their optimum sustainable population level.

Travel Prepared

The US Department of State issues travel warnings and alerts based on health and safety issues. Check the website before travel to any foreign country: https://travel.state.gov/content/travel/en/traveladvisories/traveladvisories.html.

The Centers for Disease Control and Prevention (CDC) issues travel notices for specific destinations about current health issues, including disease outbreaks, special events or gatherings, natural disasters, or other conditions that may have health implications. Find travel health notices and search by specific country on the CDC website: https://wwwnc.cdc.gov/travel/notices.

North America

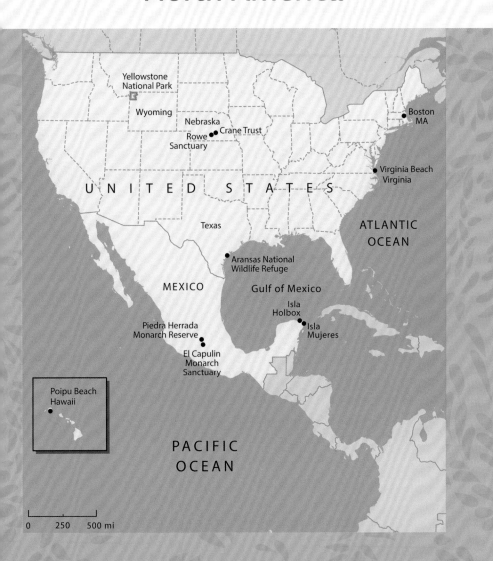

Yellowstone
National Park

Wyoming

Nebraska

Rowe
Sanctuary

Crane Trust

Boston
MA

Virginia Beach
Virginia

U N I T E D   S T A T E S

Texas

ATLANTIC
OCEAN

Aransas National
Wildlife Refuge

MEXICO

Gulf of Mexico

Isla
Holbox

Isla
Mujeres

Piedra Herrada
Monarch Reserve

El Capulin
Monarch
Sanctuary

Poipu Beach
Hawaii

PACIFIC
OCEAN

0   250   500 mi

Gray Wolf

Canis lupus

Wolves famously live in packs. These social groups number seven to eight animals, including a mated male and female, their pups, and older offspring. The female and male pair usually mate for life and lead the pack in hunting, choosing den sites, and establishing and defending territory. Pack members communicate with barks, whines, growls, and howls, and each individual has a unique howl.

Females bear an average of five pups, giving birth in April. Young come out of the den between 10 and 14 days after birth, and all members of the pack work together to feed pups, remaining at the den for 3 to 10 weeks. Young wolves may eventually disperse to find their own territory and establish a new pack, sometimes traveling as far as 500 miles from their previous home.

Wolves prey on elk, deer, and caribou, as well as rabbits and other small animals, and are not above scavenging something they find already dead.

These ancestors to our pet dogs, which come in all sizes, stand 26 to 36 inches tall at the shoulder, males weighing 100 to 130 pounds and females 80 to 110 pounds. Life is tough in the wild; a wolf typically lives only 3 to 4 years; some, though, have been known to live as long as 11 years. Having a healthy pack and a territory remote from humans helps.

In addition to gray, the most common color, these wolves sometimes have white fur in the high Arctic and black coats in the Rocky Mountains.

Once numbering some two million and ranging throughout North America, gray wolves were eliminated from 95 percent of their range by the early 1900s.

According to National Park Service biologist Doug Smith, who leads the Yellowstone Wolf Project, the last wolf in the park was killed in 1926. From 1995 to 1997, the National Park Service captured 41 wild wolves in Canada and Montana and released them into Yellowstone as part of efforts to restore these native residents. The wolves adapted well; between 2009 and 2015, the number of wolves in the park ranged between 83 and 104, and at the beginning of 2016, 10 packs totaling at least 98 wolves had territories primarily within the park.

Smith has studied the introduced wolves from the moment they arrived. He and his colleagues collar some of the wolves to track them for observation from the air and the ground. In 2013, roughly 22 percent of the animals wore collars. Scientists also analyze the carcass of most wolf kills, which requires tramping through miles of deep snow or up sunbaked slopes, depending on the season. The point of all this effort is to look at the effect wolves have on the larger Yellowstone ecosystem.

Scientists already know that apex or top predators such as wolves help make natural ecosystems healthier. In Yellowstone, the return of wolves triggered what biologists call a trophic cascade, or series of related ecosystem events.

When no wolves lived nearby, elk in the park lounged around in groups of 300 to 500, overbrowsing the landscape. The presence of wolves forced elk to behave, well, more like elk, forming herds of 10 to 12 and moving around more often to avoid becoming a meal. This normal elk behavior allowed more growth of aspen, willow, and cottonwoods, which in turn led to increases in songbirds and beaver. Ponds built by beaver colonies provide homes or food for fish, reptiles, amphibians, insects, and other small mammals. Tree roots prevent erosion along streams, which creates healthier vegetation communities, deeper streams, and cooler water.

The 8-Mile pack wolf pups
Credit: Dan Stahler, National Park Service

The population of endangered grizzly bears, magpies, eagles, and foxes also increased after wolves returned to Yellowstone. These species regularly scavenge wolf kills, making these canines sort of the pizza delivery service of the wilderness.

Wolves do not encounter livestock in the park, but individuals dispersing from their pack may. According to Suzanne Stone, a wolf expert with Defenders of Wildlife, predators in general account for at most only 5 percent of livestock loss, and wolves specifically for merely a fraction of that. Affordable, nonlethal methods have proven effective at keeping wolves and livestock apart, including temporary fencing and simply having a human stay with a herd.

Hunters often express concern that wolves will "wipe out" the park's elk. That simply cannot happen. Killing an elk or other large animal is dangerous business for wolves. Hunts often take hours and cover a lot of ground—using up a lot of precious energy—and most hunts end without a kill. A pack territory supports only so many individuals, with natural forces limiting the population. In addition, predator species cannot eliminate their prey—as a prey population declines, so, out of necessity, does the number of predators. Smith's data show that Yellowstone's wolf numbers rise and fall in tune with prey population as well as with disease, competition, and other influences. Once reestablished, Yellowstone's wolf population has ranged from fewer than 100 to as many as 170.

The wolves have made elk more vigilant and wary, so hunters admittedly have to work harder now. But wolves also cull weaker or diseased animals, so those hunters who persevere will take more beautiful and vigorous elk.

"Predation is a dominant force in ecosystems," says Smith. "As we settled this country, we eliminated most predators in the lower forty-eight and forgot how carnivores can restructure nature. The way nature evolved, predators kept herbivores at modest densities, so you had luxurious and resplendent plants that provided habitat for a multitude of animals."

Threats to Wolves

The US FWS listed the northern Rocky Mountain population of gray wolf as Endangered under the ESA in 1973 and, in 1978, listed as Endangered the entire species throughout the contiguous United States and Mexico. Exceptions included the Minnesota gray wolf population, classified as Threatened, and delisting the Northern Rocky Mountain Distinct Population Segment excepting Wyoming, which includes Montana, Idaho, eastern Washington, eastern Oregon, and north-central Utah, "due to recovery," according to FWS. The agency has proposed delisting populations in California, Michigan, Oregon, Washington, and Wisconsin.

In January 2015, some 23 organizations, including the Humane Society of the United States, Center for Biological Diversity, and Fund for Animals, petitioned the FWS to reclassify as Threatened all gray wolves in the conterminous United States, except the Mexican wolf in the Southwest. In July 2015, FWS determined the petition did not present "substantial scientific or commercial information" and declined to conduct a status review. The IUCN Red List categorizes gray wolves as Least Concern (www.iucnredlist.org/details/3746/0).

During the nineteenth and twentieth centuries, humans moved into and altered much wolf habitat and routinely slaughtered the animals, which they viewed as pests. Today, conflict over livestock remains one of the most common causes of the death of protected wolves. For populations that do not have federal ESA protection, the most common cause of death is hunting and trapping.

Habitat fragmentation and loss represent a serious threat to all gray wolves. Packs require large territories, and dispersing individuals must navigate highways, development, and ranchlands. This animal's worldwide range has decreased by about a third.

Originally the most widely distributed mammal in the world, the gray wolf became extinct in much of Western Europe, the United States, and Mexico, now remaining mostly in wilderness and other remote areas. Since the 1970s, population declines have slowed thanks to legal protection, land-use changes, and shift of human population from rural to urban areas, with natural recolonization occurring in parts of its range in addition to reintroduction in three areas of the United States. A still relatively widespread range and, for now, stable population trend mean that the species does not meet criteria for a Threatened category at the global level. At regional levels, the IUCN acknowledges, several wolf populations are seriously threatened.

Seeing Wolves in Yellowstone National Park

Yellowstone ranges from about 5,000 to 11,000 feet in elevation with a wide variety of ecosystems, including dry steppe grasslands, lodgepole pine forest, riparian zones, and alpine tundra. Yellowstone's northern range offers one of the world's best opportunities to see wolves in the wild. But the park's diversity and sheer size—2.2 million acres—make a compelling argument for guided visits. Experienced guides can improve your chances for seeing a wolf, as they know the territories and habits of these park residents.

Yellowstone Association Institute

This organization offers three options for seeing wolves in the wild, Lodging and Learning programs, Field Seminars, and private tours.

Lodging and Learning programs include Wolves in Winter, Fall and Spring Wolf and Elk Discovery, and Wildlife Watching on the Northern Range. Tours travel through the park by van, and sometimes visitors can watch wolves through spotting scopes right from the road as wolves lounge at the edge of the woods. The group also hikes or snowshoes into the landscape, looking for wolves. Fall offers near guarantees of elk sightings and the chance to see wolves hunting in deep snow, when they enjoy an advantage over heavier, less nimble prey. On these outings, participants also may see grizzly bears, bison, mountain goats, bighorn sheep, coyotes, hawks, swans, eagles, and beaver; many different flowering plants and trees; and geologic features including mud pots, hot springs, fumaroles, and geysers. Yellowstone contains the majority of all geysers in the world.

Lodging and Learning programs include in-park transportation, breakfast and a box lunch daily, dinner on the last night, guide services, and use of spotting scopes and binoculars. Spotting scopes allow observation of animals from a distance without disturbing their natural behavior. The trip includes lodging at Mammoth Hot Springs Hotel, which takes its name from steaming limestone terraces nearby and is the only lodging accessible by vehicle in winter. It offers standard hotel rooms, a suite, and four cabins with private hot tubs.

Field Seminars include Lamar Valley Wolf Week, a full-immersion experience searching daily for wolves and prey species, observing wolf behavior, exploring habitat, and learning about conservation and management of the species, all in the company of wolf experts and managers. These interactions occur both out in the field and during evening lectures on a variety of topics, including wolf communication, which may include howling. Field Seminars include daily outings, three meals daily, expert guide, and use of snowshoes and scopes or binoculars. For an additional charge, participants can stay in cabins at the Lamar Buffalo Ranch, a historic campus in the scenic Lamar Valley. Each log cabin has three single beds and propane heaters and access to a bathhouse with private showers and use of a kitchen. Cabins do not have electrical outlets or plumbing.

Private tours include a guide, in-park transportation, use of binoculars or spotting scopes, drinks, and snacks. Lodging is available in cabins at the Yellowstone Overlook Field Campus, 80 acres with incredible views of the park, kitchens, and open floor plans perfect for group activities. Camping is available throughout the park in season.

The World Wildlife Fund and Natural Habitat Adventures

This partnership offers winter wolf tours January to March in Yellowstone and Grand Tetons National Parks. The trip includes searching Jackson Hole for wildlife such as bighorn sheep, bald and golden eagles, coyotes, bison, mule deer, moose, and elk, along with a ride in a horse-drawn sleigh across the National Elk Refuge for close-up photos of its massive overwintering herd. The group travels through Yellowstone by snow coach, spending two full days searching for wolves, then visiting Old Faithful and photographing moose, river otters, and trumpeter swans. Many of the guides have extensive experience working with researchers who track these wolves daily, increasing chances of seeing them on the tour. Trips start at Jackson Hole, Wyoming, and end at Bozeman, Montana, or vice versa.

Travel Information

Yellowstone National Park: (307) 344–7381, https://www.nps.gov/ yell/index.htm

Yellowstone Association: (406) 848–2400, https://www.yellowstone association.org

World Wildlife Fund: (800) 543–8917, https://www.nathab.com/ us-national-parks-tours/yellowstone-wolves-wildlife-adventure/

Travel tips Fall is the best time of year for seeing wolves. Expect cold weather, especially morning and evening, and possible snow.

Monk seal, Hawaiian and Pacific Islands National Wildlife Refuges
Credit: James Watt, USFWS

Hawaiian Monk Seal

Neomonachus schauinslandi

Kauai, Hawaii   *Poipu Beach*

This species gets its name from folds of skin on the seals' heads that make it look like they wear a monk's hood and from the tendency of individuals to spend time alone or in only small groups. While agile in the water, they look less so on land; adults weigh in at a hefty 375 to 450 pounds and are 7 to 7.5 feet long. No wonder they mostly just lie around on the beach.

The earth once had three species of monk seals, the Caribbean, Hawaiian, and Mediterranean. The Caribbean species went extinct, and the Hawaiian is one of the world's rarest marine mammals.

Females mature around age five. Mating takes place underwater, and females give birth in late March and early April after 10 to 11 months of gestation. They seem to prefer shallow, sheltered water near sandy beaches for pupping. Newborns nurse for about a month, with the mother fasting and remaining on land with her pup during that time. Typically, physical contact occurs only between mothers and their pups or recently weaned young. Otherwise, individuals interact little, even when hanging around near each other on the shore.

Monk seals feed on fish, cephalopods, and crustaceans, hunting in the shallow waters surrounding atolls and islands, as well as at submerged banks farther offshore, diving deeper than 1,000 feet. They can become prey for tiger and Galapagos sharks.

Hawaiian monk seals appear throughout the Hawaiian Islands but reproduce mainly at six sites: the Northwestern Hawaiian Islands (NWHI) at Kure Atoll, Midway Atoll, Pearl and Hermes Reef, Lisianski Island, Laysan Island, and French Frigate Shoals. Most of the population lives within the Papah'naumoku'kea Marine National Monument, first designated in 2006 and expanded in 2016.

These seals molt annually, a process that takes one and a half to two weeks and results in loss of their entire layer of skin and overlying fur, leaving a sleek, dark gray coat underneath. Molting seals are no one's idea of photogenic; they may have runny noses and eyes and often writhe around in the sand to help remove dead skin, which has a quite unpleasant stench. But molting is a normal annual event, and the animals do not need any interference or assistance from humans.

Their Hawaiian name, *llio holo I ka uaua*, means "dog that runs in rough water." They have other names, including *'illio holo kai*, *'illio holo i ke kai*, *na mea hulu*, and *sila* or *kila*.

Threats to Hawaiian Monk Seals

In the United States, Hawaiian monk seals are listed as Endangered under the ESA and Depleted under MMPA. They are listed in CITES Appendix I and on the IUCN Red List as Critically Endangered (www.iucnred list.org/details/13654/0).

The population declined from about 1,500 in 1983 to 1,209 in 2011, only 632 of them mature individuals. The species continues to decline, mainly from limited food supplies. This may be caused by changing ocean conditions, long-term effects from commercial fisheries, or competition from other predators.

The animals likely were negatively affected by military activities at several bases in the NWHI before World War II. The military no longer maintains bases in areas where the seals live, though; in fact, most monk seals live isolated from any significant direct human contact. Permanent US FWS structures remain at Tern Island and Midway Atoll, however, and former coast guard facilities at Kure Atoll. Derelict structures, particularly at Tern Island, pose significant entrapment hazards for the seals, and chemicals and contaminants left behind may be harmful.

Current threats to monk seals also include entanglement in discarded fishing net and line and other marine debris. As sea levels rise because of climate change, seals lose land habitat, which could represent a significant threat. In the main Hawaiian Islands, the most severe threats come from hooking and entanglement in commercial and noncommercial fishing gear; boat strikes; diseases caught from feral animals, domestic pets, and livestock; and intentional killing and harassment.

Perhaps the most significant risk to the seals on Kauai is human disturbance, given the unique situation on the island where this critically endangered species comes into daily contact with people. In April 2016, for example, beachgoers took video of a man attacking a pregnant seal resting in shallow water off the beach at Salt Pond Beach Park off Kauai. The man was later arrested.

Report any harassment of monk seals at the beach, in the water, or from a boat operator to the Kauai Marine Conservation Coordinator at (808) 651-7668, National Oceanic and Atmospheric Administration (NOAA) Fisheries Office of Law Enforcement at (800) 853-1964, or local law enforcement.

Natural hazards include predation by sharks, especially on young pups, and aggression among subdominant males.

Seeing Monk Seals in Hawaii

Many Hawaiian monk seals hang around the island of Kauai. One of Kauai's most popular beaches, Poipu Beach on the South Shore, takes in two beaches separated by a tombola, a narrow sand spit that extends from shore to an island. Monk seals love to nap and sunbathe on the tombola at Poipu Beach. Their practice of coming onto the beach to nap is called hauling out.

The Kauai-based Monk Seal Watch Program focuses on protecting seals hauled out on the island's beaches and on educating visitors and residents about how to behave around them. Timothy Robinson, project coordinator for the organization, explains that the seals haul out whenever they need to rest, and some spots see more seals than others. In addition to Poipu Beach Park, seals haul out at Salt Pond Beach Park on the southwestern side and on the island's eastern side from north of Lihue to Kealia. Reaching some of the North Shore beaches involves considerable hiking.

Always stay behind barricades and signs and, in unmarked areas, at least 150 feet from these animals. Never feed the seals or interfere with them in any way. "Human behavior around them is key," Robinson stresses. "Maintain your distance, never approach them while feeding, and stay quiet. The animal's survival depends upon them getting their needed rest." The Monk Seal Watch website contains complete viewing guidelines.

Currently, no tours operate specifically for monk seal watching, but people on the many kayak, snorkeling, and catamaran tours in the area often encounter seals.

From December through May, visitors often spot humpback whales spouting off Poipu Beach and large *honu*, green sea turtles, swimming in the ocean. Restrooms, showers, and picnic tables are available at the park, which also has beach lifeguards.

The Monk Seal Watch gives weekly presentations at the Grand Hyatt in Poipu at 9:00 a.m. every Thursday morning in the Hale Nalu restaurant and monthly presentations at the Westin Resort in Princeville the third Tuesday of the month at 5:00 p.m. in the Sales Gallery, Building 1 (https://www.facebook.com/pages/Kauai-Monk-Seal-Watch-Program/100502673327911).

On the Big Island of Hawaii at Kailua-Kona, the Marine Mammal Center runs a hospital for Hawaiian monk seals. Ke Kai Ola (The Healing Sea) rescues and rehabilitates Hawaiian monk seal pups. Docents lead 45-minute tours of the center's exhibits and viewing areas, provide information on the work of the center, and tell stories about seal and sea lion patients. Tours happen daily June through August at 11:00 a.m., 1:00 and 3:00 p.m.; and September through mid-November, Mondays and Fridays at 1:00 and 3:00 p.m. and Saturdays and Sundays at 11:00 a.m., 1:00 and 3:00 p.m.

For groups of 10 or more people, e-mail learn@tmmc.org to inquire about large-group experiences, available on a limited basis and booked in advance based on educator availability. Education experts lead outreach programs on-site in Kona and throughout the community to raise awareness about the monk seal's plight.

If you spot a Hawaiian monk seal, report it to the 24-hour hotline at (808) 987-0765.

How You Can Help

You can help protect this species by observing the following practices, in Hawaii and elsewhere, and encouraging others to do so as well.

Hold On to That Balloon

Groups and individuals sometimes release helium balloons to mark joyous occasions, such as a wedding, or sad ones, perhaps a funeral or the anniversary of a loss. However, these balloons pose a serious risk to wildlife, particularly marine animals. Helium balloons rise into the atmosphere until the increased pressure inside them causes them to pop. Then they float back down and become litter. If balloons fall into the water, they may float on the surface and be mistaken for jellyfish or other food items by sea turtles, birds, and other animals—which can end up choking them. Clusters of balloon fragments and their strings can entangle marine animals.

Balloons may wash up onto beaches, as a bundle of Houston Rockets balloons once did at Ka'ena Point, Hawaii, right next to an endangered Hawaiian monk seal mother and pup. The frightened mother nipped at the balloons and moved her pup into the water, and, thankfully, the wind blew the debris farther up the beach where helpful people picked it up and disposed of it. Find more information about the harmful effects of released balloons on wildlife and the environment at https://balloons blow.org/.

Hawaiian monk seals become tangled in marine debris more often than any other marine mammal. Picking up debris on the beach and in the water helps prevent this serious problem.

Report Monk Seal Sightings

The NOAA Fisheries Service Pacific Islands Fisheries Science Center's Hawaiian Monk Seal Research Program studies the biology, ecology, and natural history of these animals. Scientists monitor and assess the six main subpopulations in the NWHI and the subpopulation in the main Hawaiian Islands, investigates threats to their survival, and works to address those threats.

If you see a monk seal, report it to the program via e-mail (pifsc.monk sealsighting@noaa.gov) or call the marine mammal response coordinator for the specific island:

Island of Hawaii: East (808) 756-5961 or West (808) 987-0765
  (24-hour hotline)
Kauai: (808) 651-7668
Maui/Lanai: (808) 292-2372
Molokai: (808) 553-5555
Oahu: (808) 220-7802

Practice Seal-Safe Fishing

If you go fishing in Hawaii, follow these practices to avoid hooking or entangling a monk seal:

- Never feed seals and avoid discarding bait or scraps into the water.
- When fishing, if you encounter a seal, stop fishing until it moves on, or change locations.

- Avoid putting things that attract seals in the water, such as fish on a stringer (use enclosed bags or sealable containers instead of stringers if possible).
- Use a barbless circle hook.
- Try not to let seals take fish off your spear, stringer, or float.

Travel Information

Poipu Beach Park: https://www.gohawaii.com/islands/kauai/regions/south-shore/poipu-beach-park

Kauai Monk Seal Watch: https://www.facebook.com/Kauai-Monk-Seal-Watch-Program-100502673327911/

Marine Mammal Center: www.marinemammalcenter.org/what-we-do/ke-kai-ola/

Travel tips Average temperatures on Kauai range between 69 and 84 degrees, with frequent but brief rain showers. Follow local restrictions on entering beaches and approaching seals.

Curious humpback whale inspecting diver
Credit: anim1087

Humpback Whale

Megaptera novaeangliae

North Atlantic Ocean

WHALE WATCH TOURS, NEW ENGLAND AQUARIUM,
AND VIRGINIA AQUARIUM

Humpback whales weigh as much as 50,000 to 80,000 pounds—even as newborns they weigh about a ton. They can reach lengths of up to 60 feet, with pectoral fins or flukes 15 feet long, which accounts for their scientific name, meaning "big-winged New Englander." These long fins give them high maneuverability despite their size, and the whales use them to slow down or even swim backward.

Primarily dark gray, humpbacks feature distinctive white patterns on their pectoral fins and belly that can be used to identify individuals.

While many humans spend the summer watching their weight, humpbacks eat as much as they can to build up fat stores or blubber that will sustain them through winter. A single whale can consume up to 3,000 pounds per day of tiny crustaceans (mostly krill), plankton, and small fish. Groups of them practice a highly complex hunting technique called "bubble netting," with each individual filling a defined role, such as distracting and herding prey or forming the "net" of bubbles near the surface.

In winter, males compete to mate with females; they chase each other, vocalize, create bubble displays, and thrash their tails and rear body, sometimes striking or surfacing on each other. Males also sing complex songs up to 20 minutes long, the sound traveling as far as 20 miles. All males in a particular population sing the same song, changing it over time.

Mothers care for newborns for up to 10 months, showing affection by swimming close to their calves and touching them with their flippers. Females typically have a calf once every two years.

This species occupies all major oceans from the equator almost to the poles. Individual population groups have specific summer feeding grounds and winter calving grounds. Seasonal migrations between the two involve great distances, farther than any other mammal. Seven animals, including a calf, completed the longest migration ever recorded, a 5,160-mile journey from Costa Rica to Antarctica. Humpbacks have been documented swimming the 3,000 miles between Alaska and Hawaii in as few as 36 days.

Mother humpback and calf, Maui, Hawaiian Island Humpback Whale National Marine Sanctuary
Credit: Sanc0612, NOAA's Sanctuaries Collection

Threats to Humpback Whales

This species has not yet been assessed by the IUCN Red List. CITES includes humpbacks in Appendix I. Humpbacks were included on the Endangered list when the ESA passed in 1973 and are listed as Depleted under the MMPA. In 2016, NOAA announced that 9 of 14 distinct population segments of humpbacks had recovered enough to not warrant listing under the ESA. Four of the distinct population segments remain Endangered, including two found in US waters at certain times of the year, and one is now listed as Threatened.

Major threats to their survival include fishing gear, strikes by large ships, harassment by whale-watch boats, loss and degradation of habitat, and hunting by humans. Entanglement in fishing gear can drown a humpback, cause serious injury, and affect its ability to swim and feed. Even whales that manage to free themselves or are freed by humans still suffer from loss of energy, stress, pain, and even reduced reproduction. For example, research has shown that entangled whales need 70 to 102 percent more power to swim at the same speed as before becoming entangled or, alternatively, must slow their swimming speed by 16 to 20.5 percent.

Whales that become entangled experience suffering that often appears to be extreme, according to Michael Moore, director of the Marine Mammal Center at Woods Hole Oceanographic Institution in Massachusetts. Whales and dolphins rank high on a scale of sensitivity to pain and suffering, he notes, and are considered as sentient and intelligent as primates. According to the MMPA, whales must be treated humanely, or in such a way that causes the least possible degree of pain and suffering. Moore believes humans have an obligation to consider the welfare of wild animals under our influence, just as we do with domesticated ones.

Changes in design of fishing gear, seasonal and geographic restrictions on certain fishing, and removal of unused gear could reduce the threat of entanglement. Fishing gear also entangles and kills or injures other marine mammals, sea turtles, sharks, and even seabirds.

Whale deaths from ship strikes have been documented in the Gulf of Maine and southeastern Alaska, and ship strikes have been reported in Hawaii. Sometimes boats bearing whale watchers even strike the animals. Whale-watch tours in New England from late spring through early fall focus on the Gulf of Maine population, particularly those within the Stellwagen Bank National Marine Sanctuary. Humpback-watching tours also are popular on the animals' wintering grounds in the Hawaiian Islands, and some operate around whales feeding in southeastern Alaska.

Humpback activity can be affected by shipping traffic, fisheries, and aquaculture as well as marine-based recreation, including resort activities and increased boating. Noise generated by oceangoing vessels, sonar used in oceanographic research, and military operations affect the whales as well.

Although the International Whaling Commission (IWC) has prohibited commercial whaling of humpbacks since 1966, Article VIII of the convention that established the IWC gives countries permission to kill whales for scientific research purposes. It also allows individual governments to set and regulate these catches. Japan has issued permits for such scientific take of humpbacks in the Antarctic and western North Pacific, setting annual sample sizes at 50 humpback whales. So far, however, the IWC reports that Japan has refrained from actually taking any humpback whales.

North Atlantic Right Whales: The Most Endangered Whale

With a population of fewer than 500 individuals, North Atlantic right whales are more endangered than humpback whales and more difficult to see. The IUCN Red List categorized the North Atlantic right whale as Endangered in 2012. These animals were listed as Endangered under the ESA in 1973 and designated as Depleted under the MMPA. The current population contains about 450 individuals.

Weighing up to 140,000 pounds and as long as 50 feet, these whales feed off the northeastern coast of the United States during summer, swimming with their mouths open to filter tiny plankton from the water with their baleen, fibrous plates hanging like mops from the roof of their mouths. Females give birth December through March in calving grounds off the coast of Georgia or northern Florida.

This species got its name because whalers considered it the "right" whale to hunt—they move slowly, float when dead, and contain enormous amounts of oil and baleen. Basque whalers began hunting these animals in the northwestern North Atlantic no later than 1530. Between 1530 and 1610, whalers may have taken thousands of right whales off Labrador and Newfoundland, while Dutch, Danish, British, and Norwegian whalers took many more. Shore-based whaling operations began along the US East Coast in the 1600s, continuing for the next two and a half centuries and removing at least 5,500 right whales and perhaps many more than that from the ocean by the 1900s.

Today, this species faces threats from habitat degradation, water pollution, whale-watching activities, and industrial noise. Climate change causes variations in seawater temperature, winds, and water currents, all of which can affect the whale's food sources.

But the most serious threat to the right whale comes from fishing-gear entanglement and ship strikes. Scientists estimate at least 72 percent of the population has been entangled at least once, and 10 to 30 percent of the population becomes entangled every year. Reported events likely represent only a portion of the toll, as we may never see many of the whales that die. The United States required fishing-gear modifications and restricts the use of certain types of gear in areas and times with likely presence of right whales. Fishing-gear rules went into effect in May 2015 (https://www.greateratlantic.fisheries.noaa.gov/protected/whaletrp/docs/2015-12869.pdf).

NOAA has tried to reduce the number of right whales struck by ships through mandatory slower vessel speeds in calving areas during season, voluntary slower speeds in specially designated areas, and aircraft surveys and alerts to ships. Moore and other colleagues have analyzed the effectiveness of measures intended to reduce vessels striking whales, including restrictions on the speed and routes of ships. Slightly shifting the location of shipping lanes and narrowing those lanes can reduce strike risk by 50 percent or more.

Using the lower jaw of a right whale, Moore and then-graduate student Regina Campbell-Malone modeled the force of a collision between a right whale and a large ship, hoping to improve our understanding of the amount of force it takes for a ship to kill a whale. They determined that whales can usually survive a collision with a vessel traveling 10 knots (11.5 mph) or less, so if ships travel that speed or slower in certain areas, strikes will kill fewer whales.

Federal law prohibits approaching a right whale closer than 500 yards without a NOAA permit or the application of one of the exemptions. This regulation covers whale-watching vessels; thus, if a whale-watching cruise spots a right whale, the boat must move away from it, so information on seeing North Atlantic right whales is not included here.

Seeing Humpbacks in New England

Two public aquarium facilities in New England that are involved in research and conservation provide guided whale-watching tours as part of their education and outreach efforts.

New England Aquarium

The New England Aquarium in Boston offers Whale Watch outings to nearby Stellwagen Bank National Marine Sanctuary aboard Boston Harbor Cruises' high-speed catamarans. The aquarium guarantees sightings of whales (although not a specific species) and provides each passenger with a free ticket on a future whale watch if none are seen. The sanctuary and surrounding waters hold several kinds of large whales, including humpback, finback, minke, pilot, and right whales. Cruisers often spot white-sided dolphins as well. Onboard naturalists trained by aquarium experts provide expert narration during the tours.

Having a prominent whale-watching area accessible from a major city presents a unique opportunity for visitors, says aquarium spokesperson Tony Lacasse. "You board a boat in Boston, and in an hour, you are in the marine equivalent of Yellowstone National Park. That is an unusual and cool experience." Humpback whales can put on a real show for watchers as they often breach, or jump out of the water, and use their pectoral fins, tails, or heads to slap the water surface.

Virginia Aquarium

Experienced naturalists guide the Virginia Aquarium's two-and-a-half-hour tours aboard the *Atlantic Explorer* to see whales, dolphins, seals, and seabirds along Virginia's coast. Educator Alexis Rabon, who leads the tours for the aquarium, says, "Our goal is to see the wildlife that visits Virginia's coastal waters in the winter, including whales, dolphins, seals, and seabirds. Each Sea Adventure lasts approximately two and a half hours, and we do not have a particular destination or direction of travel. Wildlife can be spotted at any time. We go up to twelve miles offshore, but most of our sightings occur within a closer proximity to the shoreline."

Rabon keeps her eyes peeled for large baleen whales such as humpback, fin, minke, and North Atlantic right, and small toothed whales, including bottlenose and common dolphins and harbor porpoises. She also points out harbor, gray, harp, and hooded seals and a variety of birds—common loons, double-crested cormorants, northern gannets, gulls, terns, and sea ducks. "We have the ability to observe some spectacular behaviors from these animals in their natural habitat, including feeding, communication, and social behaviors."

Humpbacks are the most commonly seen whales, and some of her favorite humpback behaviors are tail lobbing, where the animals throw their tails with a lot of force; breaching, or leaping completely out of the water; flipper slapping; and spyhopping, or positioning itself vertically with its head out of the water. Whales may do this to observe activity above the surface.

Tours are held when large numbers of whales migrate through the area's nutrient-rich waters, but migration patterns vary each year as whales follow the food. No specific trip time or month consistently offers more frequent sighting. Rabon says when water temperatures are higher, bait fish move a little closer to shore, and that tends to increase the probability of sightings. Sightings of North Atlantic right whales have happened on these whale trips, although infrequently and not in several years.

The 65-foot catamaran, outfitted especially for wildlife watching, has a heated cabin, outdoor observation decks, snack bar, and restrooms. Trips depart from a dock at the Virginia Aquarium. Proceeds from ticket sales help support the rescue and rehabilitation efforts of the Stranding Response Team and other conservation efforts at the aquarium. The aquarium also participates in Whale SENSE. Participation in this voluntary program indicates that a whale-watching company is "committed to responsible practices and whale conservation."

Travel Information

New England Aquarium, Boston: Tours April to November, (877) SEE
  -WHALE, http://www.neaq.org/exhibits/whale-watch/
Virginia Aquarium, Virginia Beach: Whale-watch tours December
  through March (depending on conditions), (757) 385–3474,
  https://www.virginiaaquarium.com/visit/Pages/Boat-Trips.aspx

Travel tip Seasickness medication may be advised.

Monarch butterflies in Mexico's monarch sanctuary
Credit: Reefs to Rockies

Monarch Butterfly
Danaus plexippus plexippus

Central Mexico

REEFS TO ROCKIES

Most schoolchildren recognize the distinctive monarch butterfly's orange wings with black veins, a thick black border, and white and orange spots. Many also can identify the caterpillar's multiple yellow, black, and white bands with two antenna-like projections on each end.

Adult butterflies have a wingspan of 3.5 to 4 inches. Males have a scent gland in a black spot at the center of each hind wing they use to attract females; these black spots help distinguish males from females. Females usually have thicker black veins on their wings than males do.

Females lay their eggs and caterpillars feed solely on milkweed plants, which contain glycoside, a toxin harmless to the caterpillar but foul tasting and poisonous to potential predators. These toxins remain even after the caterpillar undergoes metamorphosis into an adult monarch. Caterpillars create a distinctive pale green chrysalis with a row of gold dots like sealing wax. In about two weeks, an adult butterfly emerges. The adult needs some time to let its wings dry and to pump fluid into them to make them stiff before flying away.

Adult monarchs eat nectar, feeding on a variety of flowers, including milkweeds. In the process, they pollinate these plants. Monarchs also serve as food for birds, small animals, and other insects.

Monarchs show up all across North America, from Central America to southern Canada and from the Atlantic to the Pacific, wherever there is milkweed. There are actually three geographically distinct populations, one east and another west of the Rocky Mountains and one in Central America. Each has a distinct migratory pattern, with monarchs that live west of the Rocky Mountains migrating to Southern California for winter. The population east of the Rocky Mountains is famous for its migration to central Mexico, with butterflies traveling 50 to 100 miles a day and taking up to two months to complete the journey. In fact, while most monarchs live only a few weeks, the generation born at the end of the summer lives as long as eight months, overwintering in Mexico and making the journey back to the southern United States in spring.

Soon after leaving Mexico in early spring, this generation mates. Their offspring and the three or four subsequent generations continue the journey north until late summer, when the overwintering generation migrates back to Mexico and the cycle starts over again.

Threats to Monarch Butterflies

The IUCN Red List has not yet assessed the monarch butterfly species, but the organization designated the monarch migration a Threatened phenomenon in its *Invertebrate Red Data Book* in 1983 (https://www.bio diversitylibrary.org/page/31594013#page/5/mode/1up). The species is not currently listed in any of the CITES appendices.

In December 2014, US Fish and Wildlife Service announced it would review the monarch butterfly status under the ESA in response to a petition from the Center for Biological Diversity, Center for Food Safety, the Xerces Society for Invertebrate Conservation, and Lincoln Brower, professor emeritus at Sweet Briar College in Virginia. The announcement noted that on their 3,000-mile-plus migration and at their breeding and wintering grounds, the butterflies encountered many threats, including loss of habitat—particularly loss of milkweed—and death by pesticide. As a result, monarch populations have declined significantly. The agency received more than 111,000 public comments and is conducting a status review. In fiscal year 2016, FWS was preparing a five- to seven-year work plan for evaluating species, including the monarch, so did not have a time frame for completion of assessment for the monarch.

The government of Ontario, Canada, lists the monarch as a species of Special Concern, which means it could become threatened or endangered due to a combination of its characteristics and existing threats. Those threats include changes in the timing of migration and rainfall patterns in their forest habitat as a result of global climate change. Pesticides kill the butterflies and herbicides kill the milkweed they need. Research published in June 2014, for example, found that the US milkweed population fell by 21 percent between 1995 and 2013, with about 70 percent of that loss within monarch breeding areas (https://besjournals.onlinelibrary.wiley.com/doi/abs/10.1111/1365-2656.12253).

Habitat fragmentation and loss, in the United States and in Mexico, represents a serious threat to this species. Rapid development in California has affected much of the western monarch's habitat. In Mexico, monarchs concentrate in only 11 to 14 small sites. Unfortunately, the trees on which they cluster have high value as lumber. Logging not only removes roost trees but also opens up the forest canopy, which lets in snow and rain, leaving roosting monarchs more vulnerable to freezing. The government protects five sites from logging, but locals continue to remove lumber from buffer zones around these sites.

Conservation efforts continue to conflict with local economics. Despite establishment of sanctuaries in 1985 and a growing tourist trade, lumbering remains more lucrative and tourism has not created enough alternative jobs. Near El Rosario sanctuary, locals in the town of Angangueo charge visitors for transportation up the mountain, sell food and souvenirs, and charge for guided tours—but this does not as yet bring in as much income as lumber.

How You Can Help

Monarch-related tourism in Mexico provides income for the communities around the butterfly's overwintering grounds, offering an alternative to logging and other destructive practices. More tourism equals more

Monarch butterflies overwintering in Mexico
Credit: Reefs to Rockies

income and makes protecting the butterflies a better alternative to unsustainable logging.

You can help monarchs without leaving home, though, by planting native milkweed and other nectar sources in your yard and avoiding the use of pesticides. Planting milkweed species native to your particular area is important because the timing of blooms tells monarchs when it is time to migrate. Order a Monarch Waystation kit from Monarch Watch (monarchwatch.org/waystations/seed_kit.html) or ask your local natural garden store about native milkweed and other native flowering plants. The Monarch Watch kit page includes a list of species appropriate for east of the Rockies and west of the Rockies.

Another way to help is to symbolically adopt a butterfly through the World Wildlife Fund ([800] CALL-WWF, https://gifts.worldwildlife.org /gift-center/gifts/Species-Adoptions.aspx).

Seeing Monarchs in Central Mexico

Reefs to Rockies' five-day Monarch Butterflies and Magical Cities includes visits to two monarch butterfly sanctuaries near Mexico City. The trip begins in the capital city and then goes to Piedra Herrada Monarch Reserve, about an hour away. Swarms of monarchs often appear even before the group reaches the sanctuary to hike into the forest, where millions of monarchs create an orange and black carpet on the trees, clustering together for warmth. As impressive as this sight is, when the sun shines on and warms the butterflies, they fly, creating an even more impressive, brilliantly colored, fluttering cloud.

Spend the rest of the day exploring Valle de Bravo, one of Mexico's Pueblos Magicos, with narrow, cobblestoned streets and colonial-style buildings on the shores of Laguna de Avandaro.

Day three begins with a visit to El Capulin monarch sanctuary, which sees fewer visitors than Piedra Herrada and feels much wilder. "El Capulin is very off the beaten path," says Reefs to Rockies cofounder Sheridan Samano. "If the sun comes out, the butterflies warm up and fly. This mass flight is so impressive. It also is impressive to see them in the trees, but hard to photograph because they are in the shade."

The group travels El Capulin's rugged trails by horseback, led by local guides, spending time taking in the butterfly gathering and having lunch at a typical *fondita*. The tour includes multiple visits to the sanctuary, Samano adds, "because every day is different."

On the way back to Mexico City, a stop at Metepec includes learning how local artisans sculpt clay. That evening's hotel lies only a block from Mexico City's Zocalo and Historic Center, a UNESCO World Heritage Site.

Reefs to Rockies employs full-time local bilingual biologist guides, trip hosts, and local guides in addition to patronizing local restaurants and lodging facilities. Your trip fee includes entrance fees at the monarch reserves and a donation to support local conservation efforts. All of this creates economic benefit for area residents, directly tied to the presence of the monarchs and preservation of their habitat.

Reefs to Rockies notes that, to operate as a responsible tour company, it adheres to the following policies, which help preserve areas where the company operates so that these places remain available for future generations of visitors:

- Book when possible at local hotels committed to sustainability and conservation. Properties not locally owned must have a local presence and employ community members.
- Hire local guides who work to minimize environmental impact.
- Educate travelers about sustainable tourism, environmental stewardship, and resource conservation.
- Maintain small group size.
- Support wildlife conservation efforts at each destination.
- Offer carbon offset programs to travelers.
- Follow environment-friendly practices at the company office, includ-

ing energy conservation, recycling, composting, and using recycled paper products.

Travel Information

Reefs to Rockies: Monarch tours December to mid-March (peak mon-arch activity mid-January to mid-March), (303) 860-6045, http://reefstorockies.com/destinations/north-america-2/mexico/monarch-butterflies-magical-cities/

Travel tips Check the US State Department website for travel advisories. Check the CDC website for possible precautions against mosquito-borne illnesses.

Sandhill cranes viewed from Crane Trust blinds in Wood River, Nebraska
Credit: Chuck Cooper, Crane Trust

Sandhill Crane

Grus canadensis

Platte River, Nebraska

CRANE TRUST

Big Bird would feel right at home with sandhill cranes, which stand 5 feet tall with wing spans stretching up to 6 feet. These impressive birds also fly as far as 5,000 miles twice a year and mate for life. They are grayish in color with a patch of skin on the forehead that can range from a bright crimson to dull reddish-gray, a sort of facial mood ring.

Their habitat includes prairies, fields, marshes, and tundra, depending on the region. They migrate north to spend their summer on breeding grounds in the northern United States and Canada and head back south to Texas and New Mexico in winter. On the spring migration, about 80 percent of the population—some 500,000 individuals—gathers in Nebraska's Platte River Valley, something the species has done for millions of years. Lesser sandhill cranes make up the majority, but some greater sandhills join in, the two subspecies intermingling and becoming almost indistinguishable.

Sandhill trivia: adult females are called mares, adult males are called roans, and young cranes are known as colts. These birds live for 20 years, and a mated pair produces one or two eggs a season. They usually build nests near marshes or bogs out in open grassland or areas surrounded by forest. Chicks leave the nest within a day, although both parents feed the young until they learn to feed themselves. They begin to fly about 65 or 75 days after hatching but remain with their parents for up to 10 months, joining them on the epic family spring vacation.

The birds migrate primarily during the day, using thermal updrafts to rise thousands of feet in the air, then gliding downward until they catch another thermal. Average flight speeds of 45 to 50 miles per hour make it possible for them to travel up to 300 miles in a single day—500 with a good tailwind. Individual family groups gather into large flocks along the Platte, socializing, feeding, and resting.

Cranes use their long, pointed bill and their feet as protection from predators. They have a complex system for communicating, using a variety of dance steps that include bowing, jumping, stabbing with their beaks, and flapping their wings. Young birds practice their dance moves for years. Mated pairs stand close together and perform synchronized calling.

View of sandhills from Crane Trust blinds in Wood River, Nebraska
Credit: Chuck Cooper, Crane Trust

Threats to Sandhill Cranes

The IUCN lists sandhill cranes as a species of Least Concern, given its large range and a currently increasing population. The birds are listed in CITES Appendix II. Localized, nonmigratory populations in Mississippi and Cuba are Endangered.

While this species is not officially classified as Endangered under the ESA, degradation and loss of habitat at major migration stopover points pose a serious potential threat. After collecting hundreds of thousands of observations by citizen-scientists, Audubon Society scientists applied sophisticated models to predict how climate change will affect these birds. Their efforts project a 58 percent loss of this bird's current winter range by 2080.

The rare ecosystem of their impressive Nebraska gathering place also faces intense pressure. Roosting on shallow sandbars in the middle of channels of the Platte keeps the birds safe from predators. While they feed on leftover corn in surrounding fields, this does not provide minerals and proteins needed for successful reproduction. They also need to feed on a variety of invertebrates, including insects and snails, and on plant tubers that grow in nearby wet meadows and grasslands. This feeding is particularly important in spring, when the birds increase their weight by 15 to 20 percent for the breeding season. The river valley's wetlands, grasslands, and crop fields and secure roosting sites in close proximity are essential to the birds' survival.

While the spring gathering used to cover some 150 miles of the Platte River, only bits and pieces totaling about 80 miles remain suitable for the cranes. Fifteen major dams and reservoirs upstream take 70 percent of the river's water and have eliminated the periodic snowmelt flooding that swept the wide, braided river's multiple channels free of vegetation and trees. Most of the river is now narrow and deep, far too deep to use for roosting. The Crane Trust in Wood River, Nebraska, protects and maintains roughly 10,000 acres through direct ownership and conservation easements. The organization works to re-create natural influences such as wildfire through prescribed burning, river dynamics by mechanical clearing, and bison grazing, maintain a herd of genetically pure bison.

The Trust also conducts scientific monitoring and evaluation of the ecosystem and the birds and other wildlife. This research helps evaluate the effectiveness of land management practices and the status of species of concern in the area. The 300 or so critically endangered wild whooping cranes, for example, join the sandhill cranes on their migration through the valley.

Seeing Sandhill Cranes on the Platte River

The Crane Trust Nature and Visitor Center serves as an outlet for outreach and education and the starting point for seasonal tours of crane departures from the river in the morning and their return in the evening. Cranes begin arriving here in mid-February, with numbers peaking the last half of March.

Group viewing tours meet at the center before dawn for the 10-minute walk to blinds along the shore of the river. From the moment visitors step outside the center, they hear the sound of the birds waking up, individuals squawking and joining together into a cacophony that sounds like an enormous, out-of-tune orchestra warming up. From the blind, tourists watch as birds, one after the other, stretch their wings, leap off the ground, and stalk about in the shallow water. They begin to lift off, individually or a few at a time at first, then in huge waves, their noise rising as well. Once or twice, hundreds take flight at the same time, covering the sky. Finally, only a few stragglers remain in the river.

Their return in the evening looks less dramatic, with small groups of birds flying in from every direction as light fades from the sky. This experience, though, offers better chances for photographing the birds in flight and landing, and sunset becomes a dramatic backdrop.

The Crane Trust also offers on-site lodging in two four-bedroom cabins and one with two suites. Overnight stays include breakfast and dinner, an arrival reception, and morning and evening tours to the blind. Hard-core photographers can also overnight in private blinds, limited to two people. The property includes 30 miles of hiking and biking trails as well.

The Iain Nicolson Audubon Center at Rowe Sanctuary near the town of Kearney also offers morning and evening guided tours to blinds to view sandhills from early March to early April. Overnight photo viewings are available here as well. This sanctuary protects and maintains another 2,800 acres of river and surrounding habitat.

Reefs to Rockies also offers spring tours to Rowe Sanctuary to witness the sandhill crane gathering and Switzer Ranch Prairie Preserve to observe greater prairie chickens. Male greater prairie chickens gather in groups called leks on open areas of the tall- and mixed-grass prairie, where they make distinctive booming sounds and perform ritualized dances that include rapid foot stomping, jumping into the air, and sparring with their wings. Anywhere from 8 to 20 males may appear, although as many as 70 have been observed on one lek. In addition to the unique booming sound, the birds whoop and gobble and flash bright orange balloonlike air sacs on the sides of their heads. These dancing displays can last up to two hours and establish a dominance hierarchy among the birds, determining which ones will mate that year.

The Reefs to Rockies trip travels by car from Denver to Kearney, Nebraska, birding along the way and arriving at Rowe Sanctuary in time to watch sandhill cranes return to their evening roosts. Morning viewing of the cranes leaving the river to feed in the fields nearby is followed by birding along the Platte on the way to the Prairie Reserve. There, guests visit greater prairie chicken or sharp-tailed grouse leks early the next morning to observe the birds' dancing displays, followed by breakfast and a guided 4 x 4 tour of the ranch and its globally significant grasslands. A second morning at the leks wraps up the trip.

Local outfitters in McCook, Nebraska, also offer excursions to blinds on private lands to watch prairie chicken dances. Greater prairie chickens face serious threats from habitat loss and loss of genetic variance given the isolation of individual populations and the lack of natural corridors between them. However, the species currently remains numerous enough that four states allow hunting of the birds.

One subspecies of prairie chicken, the Attwater, is listed as Endangered under the ESA and found only in small portions of Southeast Texas. It teeters at the brink of extinction primarily due to loss of all but about 1 percent of its coastal prairie habitat. That habitat used to cover six million acres and supported a million birds.

At the Attwater Prairie Chicken National Wildlife Refuge, on the Texas coast near Eagle Lake, the US FWS and Texas Parks and Wildlife Department maintain habitat for the birds and release captive-bred individuals. The Houston Zoo and several other facilities in Texas raise birds for this purpose.

The refuge has a five-mile auto tour loop with kiosks and interpretive signs, and the prairie chickens sometimes can be seen on the tour along with crested caracaras, white-tailed hawks, black-tailed jackrabbits, coyotes, and white-tailed deer. Males of this species also dance in leks, and the refuge hosts an annual prairie chicken festival in early April that includes tours to view them. It also offers guided van tours the first Saturday of each month.

Travel Information
Crane Trust: (308) 384–4633, https://cranetrust.org

Iain Nicolson Audubon Center: (308) 468–5282, http://rowe.audubon
.org

Reefs to Rockies: (303) 860–6045, http://reefstorockies
.com/destinations/north-america-2/united-states
/spring-magic-in-nebraska/

McCook, Nebraska: http://prairiechickendancetours.com

Attwater Prairie Chicken National Wildlife Refuge: (979) 234–3021,
https://www.fws.gov/refuge/attwater_prairie_chicken/

Travel tip The weather can be quite cold in Nebraska this time of year, especially in the early morning.

A whooping crane family in its wintering grounds at Aransas National Wildlife Refuge, Texas

Credit: Klaus Nigge, USFWS

Whooping Crane

Grus americana

Aransas National Wildlife Refuge, Texas

VARIOUS OUTFITTERS

Whooping cranes stand nearly 5 feet tall, weigh between 14 and 16 pounds, and have wings up to 7 feet. Bright white body feathers contrast with dark black on the wing tips and a black crescent of feathers and patch of red skin on the head.

Whoopers mate for life and have a loud and elaborate courtship ritual that includes both birds calling, flapping their wings, bowing their heads, and leaping into the air. Pairs typically perform this ritual before mating in late winter, but they also exhibit similar behavior when defending their territories or playing.

One wild, natural flock of these birds remains in North America. The flock nests in spring and summer in Wood Buffalo National Park in Canada's Northwest Territories and spends winter in Texas, primarily at Aransas National Wildlife Refuge. All the wild and captive whooping cranes alive today, in fact, descended from 15 cranes that wintered in Texas in 1941.

The birds may live as long as 25 years in the wild, and those that lose a mate have been known to find another. Adult females build a nest on small islands of rushes, cattails, and sedges and lay two eggs, although the pair usually rears only one chick. During dry years, the nests are subject to heavy predation and few young survive.

In fall, the birds make the 2,500-mile flight from their Canadian nesting grounds to the Texas coast. Some white adult feathers will begin to

Whooping crane chick
Credit: International Crane Foundation

appear in the rusty-brown plumage of the juveniles at this point, and they will sport all-white feathers by spring. The cranes arrive at Aransas by December and begin eating blue crabs, wolfberries, crayfish, frogs, large insects, and acorns that have been roasted during prescribed burns, fattening up to prepare for the long trip back to Canada. They begin that journey when days get warmer and longer in the spring.

The birds may travel as a single pair or in a family group or small flock. Sometimes they join larger flocks of sandhill cranes (see the "Sandhill Crane" section to read more about the impressive migration of those birds). Whoopers migrate during the day with regular stops along the journey.

Threats to Whooping Cranes

The IUCN listed whooping cranes as Endangered in 2012, and the species was listed as Endangered under the ESA in 1967 (www.iucnredlist .org/details/22692156/0).

Prior to European settlement, North America had an estimated population of more than 10,000 of these birds. That number had declined to between 1,300 and 1,400 birds by 1870. In 1938, only 15 adults remained. The wild population totaled 385 birds at the end of 2008, with the self-sustaining population that migrates between Canada and Texas numbering 266 individuals, fewer than 250 of them mature birds.

Two populations were reintroduced in the eastern United States in 2007, a nonmigratory flock in Florida that included some 41 birds and a flock that migrates between Wisconsin and Florida, which numbered 75 birds. Neither of these flocks is yet self-sustaining. In 2011, a flock of 10 juveniles was reintroduced in southwestern Louisiana.

Overhunting, loss of habitat, and human disturbance caused the species' decline and continue to affect the birds. In the eastern population, shooting accounted for nearly one in five whooping crane deaths, among those where the cause could be determined, according to the International Crane Foundation. More than 20 have been shot and killed in the past five years.

Collision with power lines causes significant fledgling death and injury; markers can reduce theses collisions by as much as 80 percent, but most power lines remain unmarked. Increasing numbers of wind turbines installed in the migration corridor could decrease the availability of areas for the cranes to stop over during migration. The related increase in the number of power lines also could increase the risk of collisions.

Drought poses a serious threat to all habitats used by these birds, but especially on nesting grounds. Reduced fresh water flowing into coastal estuaries and wetlands, whether from drought or increased human use, leads to reduced populations of blue crabs and wolfberries, important sources of food for the birds. Coastal development, climate change–related sea-level rise, chemical spills, and human disturbance all threaten the Texas wintering grounds as well.

Aransas National Wildlife Refuge has enough space for as many as 500 birds. If the population grows larger than that, cranes would need to expand into unoccupied habitat, and much of what is available is threatened by development. Reduced flows in Nebraska's Platte River, a key stopover area for migrating birds, presents another threat. A hurricane or contaminant spill could seriously affect their wintering grounds in Texas. Some birds have been illegally shot as well.

In addition to protected lands at Wood Buffalo National Park in Canada and Aransas National Wildlife Refuge in the United States, the birds have protection at Salt Plains National Wildlife Refuge in Oklahoma, traditionally a major stopover for the migration. The Canadian Wildlife Service and the US FWS coordinate recovery efforts for the species.

Seeing Whoopers in Texas

Aransas National Wildlife Refuge takes in more than 24,000 acres of natural and managed wetlands, both salt marshes along the bays and brackish and freshwater wetlands within the Blackjack Peninsula and Matagorda Island Units. These wetlands serve as winter and breeding habitat for a variety of waterfowl, their abundant and diverse populations of insects providing an important protein source for the birds. Observers have documented more than 400 bird species on the refuge, including roseate spoonbills and all six rail species. The refuge also offers the opportunity to see alligators.

An entrance kiosk, open every day except Thanksgiving and Christmas, offers maps and exhibits. The refuge offers a driving tour, a number of wildlife-watching and nature trails, and scenic overlooks. Good places to watch for whooping cranes include a 40-foot-tall observation tower overlooking marshland and observation decks along the 1.4-mile Heron Flats trail. The cranes arrive here in mid-October and leave around mid-March. The refuge's location is remote, with only very small towns close by, so come prepared.

Whooping cranes also frequent the Matagorda Island Unit of the refuge, a 56,683-acre, 38-mile-long barrier island accessible only by boat. Other wildlife you may see on the island include endangered Kemp's ridley sea turtles, reddish egrets, alligators, and coyotes.

The national wildlife refuge posts whooping crane updates on its website while the cranes are on the Texas coast, including information from recent aerial surveys and details on habitat conditions, management challenges and successes, helpful links, and more crane-related topics.

You also can often spot whoopers at Goose Island State Park in Rockport, across St. Charles Bay from the refuge. The birds come here to feed on berries and blue crabs in the park's coastal wetlands. Visitors to Goose Island also can see nearly 300 other species of birds. One of the park's most famous residents, 1,000-year-old Big Tree, took the title of State Champion Coastal Live Oak in 1966. Although dethroned in 2003 by the San Bernard Oak on the San Bernard National Wildlife Refuge, it still rates as one of the largest live oak trees in the entire country.

Tours by boat offer the best chance to see whooping cranes up close. The *Wharf Cat* takes tours out of Rockport Wednesday through Sunday beginning around the first of December. During the 45-minute trip to the refuge, the boat passes barrier islands and coastline frequented by many species of birds, and a local naturalist on board narrates, providing details about these species as well as the whooping cranes.

The catamaran's shallow draft allows the captain to drift very close to shore, and its high observation decks provide excellent viewing of the cranes. The tour provides birding checklists, and spotting scopes and binoculars are available for rent. The boat sells food and drinks on board, and a climate-controlled cabin with viewing windows can seat up to 84 people.

On Tuesdays, *Wharf Cat* tours depart from Fisherman's Wharf in Port Aransas, about 12 miles by land south of Rockport. The scenic boat ride from Port Aransas to the refuge takes about an hour and a half. Many fishing charter boats in Port Aransas also offer trips to see cranes. This coastal town also enjoys fame as a bird-watching mecca.

Volunteer Expedition

The Earthwatch Institute has a volunteer expedition, Protecting Whooping Cranes and Coastal Habitats in Texas. This international environmental charity matches visitors with scientists conducting research around the world to work together for a sustainable environment. The organization has more than 50 research projects in a variety of locations where volunteers can help protect threatened ecosystems and keep our planet healthy.

At Aransas National Wildlife Refuge, volunteers conduct fieldwork that includes observing and documenting the whooping cranes' behavior, including foraging, defending territory, and moving between territories; collecting environmental information, including measuring surface-water quality and salinity levels; and conducting surveys of food resources available for the birds, including wolfberry fruit and other vegetation and blue crabs in saltmarsh ponds. Evenings include having dinner and listening to informal talks by the researchers, reviewing video footage from the day, and relaxing.

The research here seeks to understand the habitat value of this coastal ecosystem as part of efforts by scientists and wildlife managers to help the crane population increase from its vulnerable level to a more stable 1,000 or more.

Volunteers stay at Hopper's Landing, a rustic family-operated cabin just three miles from the refuge. Shared rooms with full, twin, and bunk beds are available, with air conditioning, full kitchens, and bathrooms. Field staff and volunteers prepare meals together, featuring local specialties, including barbecue, Tex-Mex, and seafood.

Travel Information

Aransas National Wildlife Refuge: (361) 286-3559, https://www.fws
.gov/refuge/Aransas/wildlife/whooping_cranes.html

Goose Island State Park: (361) 729-2858, https://tpwd.texas.gov/
state-parks/goose-island

Wharf Cat Tours: (361) 729-4855, http://texaswhoopers.com/

Port Aransas Charter Boats: https://business.portaransas.org/list/ql/
boating-fishing-charters-80?c=104&q=&st=3

Earthwatch Institute: (800) 776-0188, http://earthwatch.org/
expeditions/protecting-whooping-cranes-and-coastal-habitats-in-
texas#lead-scientists

Travel tips Winter weather is unpredictable in Texas. In warmer
weather, be prepared for mosquitoes. Seasickness medication may be
advised.

Central and South America

BELIZE Swallow Caye
Chan Chich Lodge Wildlife Sanctuary
Placencia

Caribbean Sea

ATLANTIC
OCEAN

Samiria
River

PERU

Barba Azul
Nature
Reserve

BOLIVIA

PACIFIC
OCEAN

ATLANTIC
OCEAN

FALKLAND
ISLANDS
(U.K.)

0   250   500 mi

Amazon River dolphin in the Samiria River at the heart of Peru's Amazon region
Credit: Pablo Puertas

Amazon River Dolphin

Inia geoffrensis

Amazon River Basin, Peru

EARTHWATCH INSTITUTE

The antics of dolphins and their humanlike intelligence make them popular with wildlife watchers. Few people have seen this freshwater species, also called the pink river dolphin because of its pale pink color. It lives throughout South America's Amazon and Orinoco River basins, where people call them *botos* or *encantados*. Native South American mythology gives these animals superior musical skill, seductiveness, and an affinity for parties. Some stories say the animals come from a utopia where they enjoy wealth without pain or death, yet they crave the pleasures and hardships of human societies. *Encantados* have magical abilities such as shapeshifting into human form, controlling storms, and enchanting humans into doing what the animals will, including transforming into *encantados* themselves and inflicting illness or death on others.

During the rainy season, when forests along the rivers flood, these dolphins hunt among the roots and trunks of partially submerged trees. They generally live in groups of two to four. Some groups live in specific areas year-round, while others move within the rivers; this mix of resident populations that remain in one area and migratory populations that move between areas occurs in marine dolphins as well.

Three recognized subspecies according to specific geographic areas include *I. g. geoffrensis* in the Amazon basin, *I. g. boliviensis* in the upper Madeira drainage, and *I. g. humboldtiana* in the Orinoco basin.

In addition to their unusual color and ability to swim in the forest, pink river dolphins have flexible necks, which allow them to move their heads from side to side. They have long snouts, rounded heads, and small dorsal fins, reaching lengths of 6 to 10 feet and weighing up to 350 pounds. They have poor vision and live in often-murky water so rely on sonar to maneuver underwater and find food, mostly fish found near the bottom of the river. The river dolphin is most closely related to the hippopotamus, not to other dolphins.

Threats to Amazon River Dolphins

The IUCN Red List previously classified this species as Vulnerable but in 2011 changed its status to Data Deficient. Data Deficient means that, while the biology of a species may be well known, scientists lack appropriate data on abundance and distribution to assess its risk of extinction. Future research may well justify a Threatened classification for this animal.

Some inhabitants along the Amazon River who see the dolphin as competition for fish, which have diminishing numbers, may chase them away, which can result in death or injury. In Brazil and Colombia, fishermen kill Amazon River dolphins to use them as bait to fish for mota catfish. Pink river dolphins also become tangled in fishing nets or struck by boats.

The Bolivian river dolphin subspecies is affected by mercury pollution caused by small-scale gold-mining activities. These particular dolphins mainly eat catfish, which are bottom feeders and pass the mercury up the food chain. Hydroelectric and irrigation dams threaten *boto* habitat, separating rivers and reducing the species' range and ability to breed.

Seeing River Dolphins in Peru

Earthwatch offers expeditions to work with researchers and villagers at Pacaya-Samiria National Reserve in the flooded Amazonian forests of northeastern Peru. Earthwatch and the Cocama people are working to-

Amazon River dolphins in the Samiria River at the heart of Peru's Amazon region
Credit: Pablo Puertas

gether on management plans that will protect the people and wildlife in the Samiria River basin, and participants help survey area wildlife and contribute data used to develop these plans.

The team travels two days along the Samiria River on a rubber boom vessel that has been restored, remodeled, and air-conditioned. The area is home to pink river dolphins as well as caimans, macaws, harpy eagles, monkeys, manatees, and giant river otters, known as wolves of the river.

"This is one of the most ecologically intact places on the planet," says Earthwatch scientist Cristina Eisenberg. "This particular spot is, to me, one of the most mythical places on earth." The tribes here never surrendered to the Europeans who took over most of the Amazon basin in the 1500s and 1600s, and, as a result, this area remains completely undeveloped. However, native inhabitants did overharvest wild animals, selling monkeys for bushmeat and killing the river dolphins because they eat fish the people wanted for themselves. That is, until scientist Richard Bodmer formed a partnership with the Cocama people to study and conserve the wildlife.

Bodmer, who holds a PhD in zoology from the University of Cambridge, has worked in this reserve for more than 20 years, with a focus on bringing together native inhabitants and government agencies to co-manage the land and wildlife. Two scientists from Peru assist with the research, as do the Cocama.

Hunting and other local practices are now more sustainably managed, but global climate change and resulting severe droughts and floods threaten the reserve. Bodmer's efforts to survey, manage, and protect the region remain critical to the wildlife and local human communities.

The project offers a variety of activities from which participants can choose, ranging from bushwhacking through the jungle to sitting in a boat. Team members may count wading birds; catch, measure, and release river dolphins; conduct daily counts of pink river and gray dolphins; or catch river fish using handmade rods and nets and then measuring, weighing, and identifying the species they catch. Other tasks include counting macaws from the boat, helping protect the eggs of river turtles, or hiking in forest areas to record movements of peccaries, tapirs, primates, and game birds. At night, teams capture caimans for measuring and then release them. Other team members work with the community, learning about local fishing and hunting and efforts to conserve natural resources. All of this collection of data provides the scientists with valuable information about the health of the ecosystem here and helps them determine whether traditional hunting and fishing levels are sustainable.

Between activities, participants can hang out on the riverboat's roof deck bar or library. Boat crew will provide short canoe excursions on request. Evening meals are served on the boat, followed by lectures, movies, and even dancing. The boat has private, air-conditioned single and double cabins with attached bathrooms. Daily midmorning coffee and afternoon tea are served, and beverages are available on the upper deck.

"This project is directly responsible for keeping one of the most important parts of the Amazon intact," Eisenberg says. "It is deep immersion; you get to see and do a lot. The dolphins circle the boat and just hang out. You get to see animals in a natural setting, acting like themselves." You can also help by making a donation to Earthwatch at http ://expeditions.earthwatch.org/contribute/.

Travel Information

Earthwatch Institute Amazon Riverboat Exploration, Peru:
(800) 776-0188, http://earthwatch.org/expeditions/
amazon-riverboat-exploration

American or West Indian Manatees, Crystal River National Wildlife Refuge, Florida
Credit: David Hinkel, USFWS

American or West Indian Manatee

Trichechus manatus

Manatees belong to the taxonomical order Sirenians, a reference to the Sirens of mythology and the fact that early European sailors long at sea confused these creatures with mythical mermaids. The animals also go by the less poetic name of sea cows. These animals can grow up to 12 feet in length and weigh as much as 1,800 pounds, not how most of us picture mermaids.

The American or West Indian manatee includes two subspecies, the Florida (*T. m. latirostris*) and Antillean (*T. m. manatus*). Florida manatees, the Florida state marine mammal, live only in the United States, although they occasionally wander to the Bahamas. The animals remain in Florida in winter seeking shelter from the cold in the southern two-thirds of Florida or at warm-water sites, including 10 power plant thermal out-falls and four major artesian springs (the head of Crystal River and Blue, Homosassa, and Warm Mineral Springs). From March to November, manatees may travel up the Atlantic coast to areas off Georgia, South Carolina, North Carolina, and Virginia. They also move west along the Gulf Coast to Alabama, Mississippi, Louisiana, and Texas. They even enter fresh water, including Lake Okeechobee and the St. Johns, Suwannee, and Caloosahatchee Rivers.

Antillean manatees live in rivers and along the coastline from the Bahamas down to Brazil, including waters of the Caribbean Sea and Gulf of Mexico. Confirmed populations still occupy coastlines and rivers in about 19 of 37 countries where the animals historically occurred.

Related to elephants, manatees have thick, wrinkled skin often covered with growing algae. They have small eyes and no outer ears but probably still have good sight and hearing. Their nostrils, located on the topside of their snouts, can close tight when underwater, and an inner membrane covers their eyeballs for additional protection. They pump their paddle-shaped tails up and down to move through the water and use two front flippers for guidance and to scoop up food.

Manatees eat mostly seagrasses and freshwater vegetation and contribute to healthy plant growth in the shallow rivers, bays, estuaries, canals, and coastal waters where they graze. An individual may consume more than 100 pounds of plants a day, typically eating 4 to 9 percent of its body weight. Manatees grab and tear plants with their lips and use the flexible upper lip to bring the food into their mouths. The American manatee has a snout that bends farther down than those of other members of the manatee family, which makes it easier for them to feed on grasses on the bottom. They use their teeth, all molars, to grind food, and as these teeth wear down and fall out, new ones replace them.

While manatees typically swim about 2 to 6 miles per hour, they can sprint at up to 15 miles per hour for short spurts and have been observed body surfing and barrel rolling. They spend their days feeding for 6 to 8 hours, sleeping between 2 and 12 hours and traveling the rest of the time. When resting, a manatee can either suspend itself in the water near the surface or lie on the seafloor. Large ones can remain submerged for as long as 20 minutes, while smaller ones may resurface every 3 to 4 minutes. Manatees squeal to communicate fear, stress, or excitement.

After 11 to 14 months of gestation, calves are born underwater and must be helped to the surface for their first breath. Calves weigh between 60 and 70 pounds and nurse under the water. Manatees live about 50 years in the wild.

Threats to Manatees

This species is listed as Endangered under the ESA and is included in CITES Appendix I. Belize's Wildlife Protection Act of 1981 lists the Antillean Manatee as Endangered. *Trichechus manatus* first appeared on the IUCN Red List in 1982 as Vulnerable. Currently, the population of mature individuals totals fewer than 10,000 with predictions for at least 10 percent decline over the next three generations. The two subspecies are listed as Endangered, each population estimated to contain fewer than 2,500 mature individuals, with both expected to decline by at least 20 percent within two generations.

Human activity poses the most serious threat to manatees, especially watercraft; collisions with boats account for about 35 percent of manatee deaths with a known cause and around 25 percent of all deaths. The number of recreational watercraft in Florida waters continues to increase along with the human population, and today boats can travel at higher speeds in shallower waters, increasing the threat to manatees and seagrass beds. Boaters often ignore slow speed zones intended to protect the animals.

In fact, of the more than 1,000 living manatees included in a photo-identification database, 97 percent bear scars from multiple boat strikes, with one-third of them severely mutilated, especially on the tail and back. Boat injuries may cause reduced breeding success or prevent some animals from breeding entirely. Recreational boat activity also may drive manatees out of areas that they prefer as well as interfere with feeding, nursing, or resting, all behaviors essential for their survival.

Loss and deterioration of habitat with warm water, including reduction in natural spring flows, also threaten Florida manatees. Manatees learned to collect around power plant warm-water discharge areas instead, but new cooling technologies have begun to replace this discharge. Losing these key warm-water sites could mean many fewer manatees in Florida. Human demand for water threatens natural warm-water artesian springs that offer manatees refuge, and ongoing development likely will continue to diminish volume and quality of spring flow.

Manatees also become entangled in fishing gear and debris, trapped in structures and pipes used for water control, crushed in structures used for flood control and canal locks, or caught between large ships and docks. Large boat traffic decreases the clarity of water and scars seagrass beds, both of which affect manatee feeding.

Ecotourism actually may pose a threat, too. Tens of thousands of people come to Crystal River, Florida, to swim with manatees, and the presence of so many human swimmers has been observed to cause changes in the animals' behavior, including decreased resting and increased swimming.

Human-caused loss of coastal wetland habitat and seagrass represents another problem for manatees. Pollution from agriculture and mining affects manatees off South American countries. Reduced water clarity affects the health and abundance of submerged aquatic vegetation, forcing manatees to travel farther, crowd together more, and forage in less-than-ideal places.

Illegal hunting, both for subsistence and profit, continues in a number of countries, including Brazil, Colombia, Costa Rica, Cuba, Dominican Republic, French Guiana, Guatemala, Honduras, Mexico, Suriname, Trinidad and Tobago, and Venezuela.

Stranding of orphaned calves represents a serious threat in northeastern Brazil, with human disturbance likely separating mothers and calves. This disturbance comes from shrimp farms, salt farms, an increase in other human activities along the coast, and poorly managed tourism. Natural threats include hurricanes, red tides, and pathogens.

Seeing Manatees in Belize

Swallow Caye (pronounced "key") Wildlife Sanctuary was established in 2002 to protect manatees. The sanctuary prohibits swimming with manatees and conducts education programs to encourage boat operators not to use motors near the manatees or speed through the area.

While many individuals and organizations supported its creation, Lionel "Chocolate" Heredia deserves most credit for the sanctuary's existence. A native of San Pedro on Ambergris Caye, Heredia started a water taxi business on Caye Caulker in the early 1970s. After visiting Swallow Caye and seeing the manatees, he decided to make it his cause to protect them. Friends of Swallow Caye organized in 2002, proving support for the idea of a sanctuary. At the same time, Janet Gibson, who completed a doctoral thesis on manatees, began a research program with the Belize Coastal Zone Management Institute. Chocolate passed away, and his wife, Annie Seashore-Heredia, continues his efforts.

Several outfitters offer day trips to Swallow Caye, including Anda De Wata Tours from Caye Caulker and Searious Adventures on Ambergris Caye. Swallow Caye is about 3 miles from Belize City, 20 miles south of Caye Caulker, and 32 miles south of Ambergris Caye.

A trip with Searious includes two snorkel stops, island hopping, and a beach cookout. It is a 60-minute boat ride from San Pedro to Swallow Caye, passing through Hol Chan Marine Reserve, where you may see sea turtles and other marine life. The boat stops at the Swallow Caye Ranger Station, a small building on stilts in about six feet of water, with manatees painted on its sides. Sometimes, based on funding, park rangers staff this station and collect a five-dollar (US$) park fee from each person on the boat.

The captain turns off the boat engine and poles through calm waters around the mangrove caye, looking for signs of manatees, perhaps their noses poking out of the water when they come up to breathe or pieces of seagrass floating in the water. The boat stops at nearby Goff Caye, a 1.2-acre island shaded by coconut trees with a palapa and picnic tables, for lunch, time on the beach, and snorkeling. After lunch, the group returns to Swallow Caye to look for more manatees; then stops at the Aquarium, a snorkel site known for rays and sharks; then at Caye Caulker, a four-mile-long island with a small cut separating northern mangrove swamps from a small village with shops, restaurants, and sandy beaches. The tour returns to Ambergris Caye by late afternoon.

Anda De Wata trips depart Monday through Friday from Caye Caulker to observe manatees at Swallow Caye and then stop at tiny Goff Caye for snorkeling and beach time while guides prepare a fresh barbecue fish lunch. Tours include no more than eight people and last from 9:30 a.m. until about 4:30 p.m.

"We see manatees ninety percent of the time, typically anywhere from two to six per sighting," says Anda de Wata's Kathrina Morera. "But I do ask that all our clients keep in mind that the animals are in their natural habitat, not caged or enclosed in any way."

Belize has named additional sanctuary areas that protect manatees and other marine life, including Southern Lagoon Wildlife Sanctuary, Bacalar Chico National Park and Marine Reserve, and South Water Caye Marine Reserve. Belize was one of the first countries in the Caribbean with a national stranding network established to rescue and rehabilitate manatees. The Coastal Zone Management Authority and Institute of Belize manage the network and conduct research on manatees (www .coastalzonebelize.org).

How You Can Help

Support Friends of Swallow Caye, the organization instrumental in establishment of the sanctuary (http://swallowcayemanatees.org/index. html).

Travel Information

Searious Adventures, Ambergris Caye: http://seariousadventuresbelize. com/manatee_snorkeling_tour.html

Anda De Wata Tours, Caye Caulker: http://snorkeladw.com/ manatee-madness-tour/

Travel tips High season is January to April. Rainy season runs June to November; hurricanes are possible July to October. November to May is warm and sunny. Check CDC recommendations for precautions against mosquito-borne illnesses.

Blue-throated macaws, Barba Azul Nature Reserve
Credit: Sebastian K. Herzog, Asociación Armonía

Blue-throated Macaw

Ara glaucogularis

Bolivia

BARBA AZUL NATURE RESERVE

This large and striking parrot sports bright plumage—turquoise-blue on its head, back, and wings with a bright yellow belly and blue cheeks and throat. It has a dark bill, yellow eyes, and a long, elegant tail. Males and females share a similar appearance, while immature birds have brown eyes and paler turquoise feathers.

Most parrots make a lot of noise, and macaws are no exception. They emit loud, raucous calls or squawks when alarmed, squawk at each other while roosting, and have a distinctive flight call. These birds can fly as fast as 35 miles per hour.

This species pairs for life, and a pair nests from November to March, using the cavities of large trees, especially palms, and lays one to three eggs. Eggs hatch in about 29 days, and the birds fledge in four months but may spend up to a year with their parents. Most frequently found in pairs, the birds do form small groups of seven to nine birds—one large roosting group of 70, most likely nonbreeding birds, has been observed. Macaws may live up to 80 years.

Every year, seasonal rainfall and meltwater from the Andes flood the Beni savanna in northern Bolivia, creating an ecoregion of palm-forested islands where motacu palms grow. Blue-throated macaws depend on this palm, feeding primarily on its nuts along with other nuts and seeds.

Endemic to Bolivia, this species now is extremely rare, with a small, fragmented range only in the northern part of the country.

Threats to Blue-throated Macaws

The blue-throated macaw became listed as Endangered under the ESA in 2013. The bird is listed as Critically Endangered on the IUCN Red List and included in Appendix I of CITES (www.iucnredlist.org/details /22685542/0).

Probably fewer than 300 blue-throated macaws remain, spread across an area almost twice the size of Texas. During the 1980s, more than a thousand wild birds were caught and exported for the international pet trade, and collecting wild birds for this trade continues to be a serious problem. This illegal trade continues, ironically, because their rarity makes the birds even more desirable to collectors. The birds were thought to have disappeared from the wild until their rediscovery in 1992. Full-time guards could stop collection, but the birds range mostly on private ranches.

Many suitable nesting sites have been lost due to practices such as burning palm grove understory, clearing for pasture, and cutting trees for fuel and fence posts on ranches. These practices also inhibit palm regeneration. The birds must compete with other macaws, toucans, bats, and large woodpeckers for limited remaining nesting sites, and blue-throated macaw reproduction also suffers from disturbance by mammals and human activity.

While the birds spend about six months foraging and roosting in the protected reserve, most do not breed there but disperse widely throughout the region. To breed successfully, the birds need trees with large trunk cavities for nests, located on isolated forest islands that protect the birds from climbing predators. Unfortunately, 150 years of intensive cattle ranching cleared most suitable old-growth, large trees.

Nest failure also occurs as a result of disease, predation, botfly infestations, and extreme weather events. Toco toucan, crane hawk, great horned owl, and southern-crested caracara prey on nestlings, and indigenous peoples hunt the birds for feathers used in headdresses. Increas-

Blue-throated macaws perching at Barba Azul
Credit: Sebastian K. Herzog, Asociación Armonía

ing fragmentation of the population causes inbreeding, which further reduces reproductive success.

How You Can Help

Do not buy these or any other exotic birds or wildlife, even from breeders. While some captive breeding occurs, it is difficult to know an individual bird's origins, and captive breeding provides cover for illegal trade. Report online listings for sale of macaws to managers of the offending website, as such trade is regulated under CITES. Those who observe physical sales, such as in markets, may report it to local law enforcement, but only if this can be done safely. People traveling in Asia can download the Wildlife Witness phone app and use it to safely report wildlife crime (https://www.wildlifewitness.net/).

Individuals also can donate to TRAFFIC, a nongovernmental wildlife trade–monitoring network that works globally to stem trade in wild animals and plants and to protect biodiversity conservation and encourage sustainable development (www.traffic.org/).

Seeing Macaws in Bolivia

Barba azul is the Bolivian name for blue-throated macaws. The 27,000-acre Barba Azul Nature Reserve is the only sanctuary for this bird and the only place within Bolivia's Beni department that provides them with suitable habitat that is free of cattle and contains old-growth, natural tallgrass savanna. Other Barba Azul residents include maned wolf, giant anteater, jaguar, puma, and marsh deer and endangered birds such as cock-tailed, black-masked, streamer-tailed, and sharp-tailed tyrants and long-tailed reed-finches. A list of 240 bird species observed at the reserve is available at http://birdbolivia.com/Barba_Azul_Nature _Reserve_Bird_List.html.

The Loro Parque Fundación and Armonia, Bolivian partner of BirdLife International, helped establish the reserve after more than 70 macaws were discovered nesting here in 2007. The reserve protects blue-throated macaws from livestock, and its field station provides logistical support to researchers studying them. In Barba Azul East, researchers study pressures related to cattle, while cattle have been removed from Barba Azul North for controlled fire experiments and studies of species diversity.

Work by Armonia and Loro Parque increased awareness among local communities and resulted in widespread condemnation of illegal trade, which most Bolivians now consider shameful. Bolivia declared blue-throated macaws as a national heritage species in 2014, which provides greater legal protection for the birds. Education and outreach efforts also have led to increased substitution of artificial feathers and other elements for real macaw feathers as decoration in traditional native headdresses. Previously, ceremonial headdresses worn by indigenous communities for cultural dances contained the two central tail feathers from as many as 10 macaws, which were killed in the process.

The project installs nesting boxes on Tiniji River forest islands in an effort to establish a breeding site within the protection of the reserve. Birds already roost on these islands, and organizers hope macaws will eventually accept the boxes as nest sites. These intelligent birds learn much of their behavior from their parents and other birds, so once one pair of macaws uses the boxes, others should copy them. In September 2016, the reserve tallied a total of 118 birds, including many juveniles, a new record. In February 2017, an expedition located a previously unknown breeding ground.

Barba Azul has a field station for staff and visiting researchers and students that also can be used by tourist groups. It has room for up to eight people in four shared bedrooms with two bathrooms. The reserve also offers four rustic, two-person cabins with private bathrooms overlooking the Omi River. A three-night stay costs $450 per person, which includes three meals a day, boat rides, and horseback riding.

Dry season from May until the end of September or early October is the best time to visit. Flights can be chartered from Trinidad to the reserve for up to five people at a time. During the dry season, visitors regularly see groups of 30 to 70 blue-throated macaws mixed in with the more common blue-and-yellow macaw. In the late afternoon, mixed flocks of hundreds of macaws can be seen flying to roosting sites.

"The birds are very easy to see and often very close," says reserve coordinator Tjalle Boorsma. "We saw one hundred seventy-nine bird species in one day in four different habitats within the reserve. An experienced guide makes seeing these birds more interesting, as each species has its story. The majestic blue-throated macaw is amazing to see, but the story behind this species is even more interesting."

Boats offer the best way to observe wildlife, and the reserve has a five-person boat with a silent outboard motor and two canoes for visitors to paddle along the Omi River. Four horses are available for exploring the savanna. Spanish-speaking Barba Azul rangers guide visitors to the best areas of the reserve to see wildlife, and professional, English-speaking guides can be arranged at additional cost through Armonía.

Tourism is one of Barba Azul Nature Reserve's main strategies to achieve economic self-sufficiency and ensure the long-term sustainability of the conservation project. In addition to visiting the reserve, people can help by donating through the website. Donations support nesting box installation and nationwide education programs to counter continuing illegal trade in the birds. People who donate on a regular schedule become Friends of Barba Azul and receive quarterly reports on activities at the reserve.

Travel Information

Barba Azul Nature Reserve: http://armoniabolivia.org/wildlife-and-bird-watching-holiday-in-boliva/

Travel tip Check CDC recommendations for precautions against mosquito-borne illnesses.

Jaguar with uncommon black coloration, a color morph found only in Central and South America
Credit: Ron Singer, USFWS

Jaguar
Panthera onca

The largest cat of the Americas, jaguars can weigh 200 pounds, smaller only than lions and tigers. The only member of the genus *Panthera* still living in the Western Hemisphere, these cats historically ranged from the southwestern United States through the Amazon basin to Argentina's Rio Negro.

Jaguars could hardly be called picky eaters, preying on peccaries, capybaras, agoutis, deer, opossum, rabbits, armadillos, caimans, and even green sea turtles. Their exceptionally powerful jaw bites with the strongest force of all the big cats; this allows them to bite through a turtle's shell as well as the skulls of larger animals, making a fatal bite between the ears directly into the brain. These cats also possess superior ambushing abilities, capable of leaping into water after prey and of carrying a large kill while swimming. They have been known to haul kills as large as a heifer up into trees to avoid floodwaters.

Unlike most cats, jaguars love water and prefer habitats with plenty of it, such as rainforest and seasonally flooded swamp areas, but in Belize, most of them prowl lowland areas with relative dense forest cover and permanent sources of water. They have been reported at elevations as high as 9,800 feet.

Jaguars have a pattern of spots unique to each individual. The spots on their head and neck are generally solid and may merge into a band on the tail, but on the body the spots are actually a flower shape called rosettes. One indigenous myth says the shape of the spots resulted from jaguars daubing mud on their bodies with their paws. Its spotted coat makes the jaguar look like a leopard, but jaguars are larger, stronger, and more muscular. Some jaguars have melanism, or darkly pigmented fur, which makes them look entirely black, but on close examination, spots are still visible.

Jaguars, lions, and tigers are the only cats able to roar, using a specialized larynx and flexible bone in the throat to produce this impressive sound. The cats roar to stake territory, communicate, or express anger. Jaguars mostly remain solitary, coming together only to breed. Mating occurs year-round, gestation lasts 90 to 110 days, and litters generally contain one to four kittens. They stay with their mother about a year or a year and a half. These animals live about 12 years.

Threats to Jaguars

The IUCN Red List categorizes jaguars as Near Threatened, and they are listed in CITES Appendix I (www.iucnredlist.org/details/15953/0). The species became listed as Endangered under the ESA in 1997.

Taxonomists recognize eight subspecies of jaguar, but genetic and body analysis provides no support for this. Jaguars at the northern and southern extremes of the species' range exhibit the most differences. Evidence exists for classifying four somewhat isolated groups in Mexico and Guatemala, southern Central America, northern South America, and in South America south of the Amazon River. Jaguar populations in Colombia are somewhat isolated from other populations by the Andes Mountains.

Jaguars once roamed an estimated 3.38 million square miles but now occupy only about 46 percent of that historic range. Most current jaguar habitat, found in the Amazon rain forest, is actually relatively poor. Very few if any jaguars remain in northern Brazil, Argentina's pampas scrub grasslands, or anywhere in Uruguay.

In the early 1900s, the US government paid bounties in some states of up to $5 per jaguar, equivalent to about $123 today. The species was listed in 1972 as Endangered under the Endangered Species Conservation Act, which was a precursor to the current ESA. The government's predator control programs had proved so effective at removing jaguars that the species was placed on the list of foreign endangered species and not listed under the ESA until 1997. The previous year, two separate jaguar sightings occurred in southern Arizona.

In March 2014, the US FWS designated as critical jaguar habitat approximately 764,207 acres within Pima, Santa Cruz, and Cochise Counties in Arizona and Hidalgo County in New Mexico. The designation excluded more than 78,000 acres of Tohono O'odham Nation lands; the tribe partners with the FWS to conserve habitat for jaguar and other listed species on its sovereign land. The designation also excluded nearly 16,000 acres on Fort Huachuca, as that facility's Integrated Natural Resource Management Plan includes conservation of the jaguar.

This species still faces threats from habitat loss, human poaching of animals it depends on for prey, and, in some portions of its range, habitat fragmentation. It has previously been listed as Vulnerable by the IUCN and will likely qualify for that status again in the near future. Deforestation continues at a high rate in Latin America, which leads to habitat fragmentation and isolation of jaguar populations and makes them more vulnerable to human interference. People in Latin America hunt the same animals that jaguars take for prey and sometimes even shoot the cats themselves, despite protection. Wild prey has been depleted on nearly a third of jaguar range, which can lead jaguars to kill cattle and then be killed by ranchers.

Anti-fur campaigns in the 1970s and implementation of CITES controls, which shut down international markets, significantly reduced commercial hunting and trapping of jaguars for their pelts, but demand remains for jaguar paws, teeth, and other products.

Seeing Jaguars in Belize

Reefs to Rockies offers customizable trips to see jaguars in Belize. Travelers stay at Chan Chich Lodge in northwestern Belize on 130,000 acres of a private nature reserve, at the heart of what is known as La Selva Maya.

Chan Chich opened in 1988, built with trees harvested and processed on-site and posts, sticks, and thatch from the surrounding jungle. It has two thatched-roof casitas that sleep three each, 12 individual thatched-roof cabanas, and a two-bedroom villa. The reserve holds abundant wildlife and provides one of the best chances to see these elusive cats in their natural habitat.

Generally, trips include three days in this location, where guests can choose from a variety of optional activities, including birding, night walks or drives, canoeing, fly fishing, and horseback riding. More than nine miles of well-maintained and marked trails lace the property, and guests can explore these on their own or on guided walks with resident experts. These include archaeological walks focusing on the former Mayan community known as Chan Chich (Little Bird); birding walks to look for some of the hundreds of resident and migrant bird species; and medicinal plant walks to learn about plants the Maya used for their healing properties.

This can be followed by two nights at Maya Center Village, a small Mopan Maya village, with a guided night hike and a half-day guided trip at Cockscomb Wildlife Sanctuary and Jaguar Preserve. This 150-square-mile nature reserve in south-central Belize's tropical forest and the eastern slope of the Maya Mountains, founded in 1990, is the world's only jaguar preserve.

The name comes from Cockscomb Mountain ridge on the northern edge of the reserve, which resembles a rooster's comb. Ancient Maya lived in this area as early as 10,000 BCE. British explorers arrived in 1888, and logging of cedar and mahogany began in 1927, continuing until 1984. Scientists Alan Rabinowitz and Archie Carr identified the basin as important jaguar habitat and convinced the government to establish a no-hunting zone, which it then twice expanded. This land provides protection for the tropical forest as well as upper watersheds of two river basins: the East Basin, which drains into South Stann Creek; and the West Basin, draining into Swasey River, a tributary of Monkey River.

The reserve contains spectacular waterfalls, mountain views, nature trails, many neotropical birds, and hundreds of species of plants, insects, mammals, reptiles, and amphibians. The Belize Audubon Society has several cabins, a house, and campgrounds available for overnight stays in the reserve.

At both locations, night walks or drives offer the best chance to see a jaguar. This is not an opportunity for a selfie to show off on social media —the darkness precludes impressive photographs—but a chance for an unforgettable encounter with a wild jaguar in its element, hunting in the dark. Other nocturnal wildlife that may be seen includes tarantulas, tree frogs, owls, kinkajous, and margays.

Belize has some of the highest biodiversity in the world. It is also an English-speaking country, which makes it a comfortable destination for people who have concerns about foreign travel.

Sheridan Samano, one of the founders of Reefs to Rockies, is a wildlife biologist by training, and fieldwork made her intimately familiar with wildlife ethics. "We find guides who pay attention to those ethics, and we continually vet itineraries, returning year after year to see whether we have had an impact. The only way conservation tourism works is if people in the area are making money, so we go to local restaurants, local hotels, so the money goes into that community. It is an incentive for people to continue doing this." Community residents understand that if they cause harm to wildlife or habitat, it directly affects their ability to make a living.

The package includes accommodations, round-trip flight from Belize City International Airport to Chan Chich Lodge, meals and guided tours, and a donation to support local conservation efforts made on behalf of each participant.

Travel Information

Reefs to Rockies: (303) 860-6045, http://reefstorockies.com
/destinations/central-america/belize/belize-wildlife-adventure/

Travel tips Peak season is from December to May. Wet season runs
June to November, but animals often are more active after rains. The
lodge is closed in September. Expect cool mornings and hot afternoons.
Check CDC recommendations for precautions against mosquito-borne
illnesses.

Southern rockhopper penguin in the Falkland Islands
Credit: Mary Curry, Adventure Life

Southern Rockhopper Penguin

Eudyptes chrysocome

Falkland Islands

VARIOUS OUTFITTERS

A crest of spiky black feathers jutting from the top of their heads, red eyes, and long yellow plumes behind each eye gives these penguins a distinctive look. Given their size—the smallest penguins at 18 inches tall and 5 to 10 pounds—maybe they feel the need to stand out.

Penguins in general have some pretty strange characteristics—birds, yet flightless, more agile in the water than many creatures that live there. Their ability to swim through frigid waters with ease hinges on highly specialized feathers, each of them short and broad and all tightly spaced to create a waterproof barrier for their skin. The shaft of each feather has tufts of down that help insulate penguins from the cold water.

Penguin wings work like flippers, with a paddle shape, flat bones, and an elbow-wrist joint almost fused to form a tapered, flat appendage, all covered in short, scalelike feathers—a design perfect for swimming. Penguins move through the water by flapping their wings. Penguins spend about 60 percent of their lives at sea; they see better beneath the surface than in the air and can even drink seawater.

Their short, strong legs sit far back on the body to make them more streamlined while swimming. Penguins stand vertically and walk upright because of this placement, taking short hops or steps, sometimes using their bills or tails for assistance on steep climbs. Rockhopper trivia: Of the 18 penguin species, only southern rockhoppers enter the ocean feet first rather than diving in headfirst.

Beginning in late summer or fall, these penguins spend three to five months at sea, foraging for krill, squid, and fish. As their name suggests, they nest and raise their chicks on rugged, rocky islands scattered within subantarctic and southern temperate regions in the Indian and South Atlantic Oceans, including the Falkland Islands and other islands off southern Argentina, Chile, New Zealand, and South Africa. The birds return to the same site each year to breed, making nests in high grasses and even using a nest again when possible. Some breeding colonies grow as large as 100,000 birds. Mating begins in October with eggs laid in November. Females may lay two eggs, but the first, smaller egg usually does not hatch. Males incubate the eggs for four months, another unusual characteristic of penguins, fasting or relying on the female for nourishment. Chicks hatch after about 33 days of incubation and are born without the yellow crests on their heads.

Southern rockhopper penguins in the Falkland Islands
Credit: Naeyshae Morgan, Adventure Life

Rockhoppers live, on average, 10 years. Their natural predators include blue sharks, leopard seals, and sea lions, along with introduced ones such as cats, rats, and pigs. Eggs and chicks may be eaten by skuas, giant petrels, gulls, and birds of prey.

Threats to Penguins

The southern rockhopper penguin is listed as Threatened under the ESA. It is on the IUCN Red List as Vulnerable. *E. moseleyi*, the eastern rockhopper penguin, is not listed (www.iucnredlist.org/details/22735250/0). Rockhopper penguins are not in any CITES appendices.

Populations in Chile and Argentina may have increased, but all other subpopulations have severely declined: an estimated 1.5 million pairs lost from Campbell Island between 1942 and 1986, 94 percent of the original total, and a drop in the Falkland Islands population of around 1.4 million pairs between 1932 and 2005. Scientific surveys indicate that, within three generations, or less than 40 years, the number of southern rockhopper penguins declined by more than a third. A variety of causes drive current population declines.

Egg collection, common until the 1950s at some colonies such as in the Falkland Islands, is now prohibited. Penguins also historically were used as bait in crab pots at a number of sites, and this, combined with collection of zoological specimens, decimated some populations. Grazing animals have caused significant vegetation loss on some islands, which affects the penguin's ability to nest successfully. A massive growth of algae, known as a harmful algal bloom (HAB), caused significant penguin mortality in the Falklands in 2002 and 2003. In Patagonian coastal waters, exploring and drilling for oil and gas pose a threat.

Large fishing operations have drastically reduced populations of fish that penguins need to survive. Warming of ocean waters caused by climate change may decrease prey availability around penguin habitats by reducing productivity or causing changes in food web structure. For example, penguins face competition with and predation by rapidly increasing fur seal populations.

How You Can Help

Make ocean-friendly seafood choices. Fishing operations represent one of the major threats to these and other penguins, so the choices you make when eating seafood can help protect them. A number of organizations offer seafood guides; one of the most respected is the Monterey Bay Aquarium's Seafood Watch. It offers a smartphone app, a search function on the website, and printable guides specific to different regions. Foods are placed in one of three categories:

- *Best*, which includes choices from well-managed fisheries and caught or farmed in ways that cause little harm to habitats or other wildlife
- *Buy*, meaning it is an acceptable choice, but some concerns exist with how it is caught or farmed
- *Avoid*, referring to seafood that is overfished or caught or farmed in ways that harm other marine life or the environment and that should not be purchased

As consumers, we play an important role. When you visit a grocery store or restaurant, ask whether it sells sustainable seafood. This question can help shape demand for and supply of fish caught or farmed in environmentally sustainable ways.

Seeing Rockhoppers in the Falkland Islands

The Falkland Islands archipelago consists of many small and two main islands, East Falkland and West Falkland. The former is home to the capital and largest town, Stanley. Commercial flights from South America and government flights from the United Kingdom land here, and some South American and Antarctic cruises stop at the islands. The Falkland

Islands Government Air Service (FIGAS) offers flights to 29 destinations throughout the archipelago from Stanley Airport.

October through March is the best time to travel here to see penguins. Rockhoppers breed at 35 colonies in the Falklands, arriving in late September or early October and leaving by the end of April. Some remain relatively close by the rest of the year, but a tracked penguin once traveled a total of 1,324 miles in 75 days (http://www.falklandsconservation.com /wildlife/penguins/rockhopper).

A number of spots on the main and smaller islands offer places to see rockhoppers along with other types of penguins and wildlife. Bleaker Island, in the southeast of the archipelago, has rockhopper as well as Magellanic and gentoo penguins, a large imperial cormorant colony, southern giant petrels, the flying steamer duck, and sea lions. The island offers many walking paths, and its long, sandy beaches sport beautiful views. The land north of the small settlement on Bleaker, listed as an Important Bird Area, is a national nature reserve.

The island offers a guesthouse that sleeps eight and a two-bedroom cottage. "Our rockhopper colony, about eight hundred fifty breeding pairs, is a fifteen-minute walk from the accommodation, very convenient," says Mike Rendell of Bleaker Island Farm. "We can offer a guided tour for orientation purposes, but you should be OK on your own thereafter. Hatching takes place from early December."

Cape Bougainville on the northern coast of East Falkland Island, approximately two hours from Stanley, has rockhopper penguins, sea lions, and southern giant petrels. Part of Gibraltar Station and owned by the same family since the 1800s, the Pitalugas, this area is accessible by road and track, or trail. Visitors must have a tour guide during summer months, and overnight camping requires special arrangement.

Kidney Island, a 30-minute boat journey from Stanley, requires a permit for landing and a local guide. Dense, high tussac grass covers most of the island, providing a haven for rockhoppers as well as other small birds, including an endemic species, Cobb's wren. Other wildlife seen here includes sea lions, Commerson's and Peale's dolphins, Magellanic penguins, sooty and great shearwaters, and white-chinned and gray-backed storm petrels. Evening cruises offer a chance to observe the sooty shearwaters.

Port San Carlos settlement on East Falkland Island, two hours northwest of Stanley, offers dramatic mountains, beaches, and shorelines peppered with rockhopper penguin colonies. Visitors can see a variety of wildlife, including king penguins, on one-mile Paloma Beach. Racepoint Farm offers accommodations in a two-bedroom house and coast tours. Camping is also available.

Port Stephens lies on the extreme southwest of East Falkland Island, roughly a one-hour flight from Stanley. Rockhopper and gentoo penguins use its rugged landscape as a breeding ground. Walks along the coast offer scenic views of the shoreline and sightings of wildlife such as sea lions, fur seals, and birds. Port Stephens Farm offers a small self-catering cottage (meaning guests bring their own food). The rockhopper colony is about an hour's walk from the settlement, or just under three miles.

Pebble Island, a 40-minute flight from Stanley, is named for translucent stones found on its beaches. More than 40 bird species call this island home, including rockhopper, gentoo, macaroni, and Magellanic penguins; imperial cormorant; and black-necked swans and other waterfowl. Wetlands and large ponds on the eastern end harbor many waterfowl and wading birds. Elephant seals can be seen on the beaches here as well. A small settlement occupies a narrow neck of land in the middle of the island, near a four-mile-long sandy beach sometimes used as an airstrip.

Adventure Life offers eight-day guided trips to the Falklands that include three days on Pebble Island as well as an overnight on Sea Lion Island and two days in Stanley. A full-day guided excursion from there goes to Volunteer Point on East Falkland Island's northern end, home to the Falkland's largest king penguin colony. Several other species of penguins also inhabit the white sandy beach and turquoise waters, along with a variety of other wildlife and spectacular scenery. This tour originates and ends in Chile.

Trip planner Mary Curry notes that the Falklands have plentiful wildlife and few visitors. "Sometimes the only people living on these islands are our hosts, and they have lived there their whole lives. They show you around and then you have free time; you can sit and observe the penguin colony all day if you want. There's not a lot of structure; it's just, let's go and appreciate this beautiful wildlife."

On Pebble Island, for example, there are seal and albatross colonies in addition to several colonies of different species of penguins, and visitors can just wander around and see them. "If you sit down about fifteen feet away from the penguins, they will start ignoring you," Curry says. "Then they'll come right up to you, and you can get great pictures without a zoom lens."

Rockhoppers, which she calls adorable with their goofy faces, hang out on rocks and boulders, true to their name. Gentoos prefer beaches and flat areas; kings, the beaches; and Magellanics, the muddy hillsides. Sometimes these various areas are within 100 feet of each other, and visitors can sit and see them all at the same time.

People who visit late in the season, from late January through March, will see penguin chicks. King penguin chicks are furry brown blobs that look like teddy bears, Curry says, and rockhoppers have little furry fluff balls for chicks. Late in the season, penguins begin molting as well.

A visit to the Falklands offers a unique cultural component, she adds. "You have British people who have been there for six generations. They are distinctly British in many ways, and their products are from Britain, but everything has a Falkland feel to it. For example, for breakfast you may have really good English biscuits and jam."

Adventure Life focuses on what general manager Jonathan Brunger calls conservation travel. "Travelers learn about the culture and places and ecosystems that need to be protected," he says. "We look for ways to support sustainable economic development, ways for local people to make a livelihood. Sustainable tourism has long-term positive effects."

Travel Information

Bleaker Island: http://bleakerisland.com/index.html

Cape Bougainville: Tour guide information Falkland Islands Tourist Board, +500 22281, https://www.falklandislands.com/ or the Pitaluga family, +500 31193

Kidney Island: Information on permits and local boat operations, Environmental Planning Department, +500 28480

Port San Carlos: Racepoint Farm +500 41012, jhjones@horizon.co.fk

Port Stephens Farm, +500 42307, par@horizon.co.fk

Adventure Life: (800) 344-6118, https://www.adventure-life.com/ falkland-islands/tours/1132/wildlife-week#overview

Whale shark in the Gulf of Mexico
Credit: Cancun Convention and Visitors Bureau

Whale Shark

Rhincondon typus

Yucatán Peninsula, Mexico, and Belize

REEFS TO ROCKIES

It's not a whale; it's a shark. A very large shark. Whale sharks can grow longer than 50 feet. Hence the "whale" in their name, even though they belong to the same class, Chondrichthyes, and subclass, Elasmobranch, as a number of other shark species.

Fortunately, while these sharks are huge, their teeth are not. In fact, they eat primarily plankton—the small animals, plants, and microbes drifting on currents in the ocean—swimming slowly with their mouths open, sucking in seawater and passing it through a structure in their gills to filter out the bits of food. While most often seen feeding this way at the surface, whale sharks can dive as deep as 4,500 feet and also eat small squid and other creatures in addition to plankton.

Generally solitary in waters around Australia, India, and the Philippines, whale sharks gather in large feeding groups at several locations around the world, including off southern Belize in spring, to feed on fish spawn, and near Mexico's Yucatán Peninsula in summer, when nutrient-rich waters carried up onto the continental shelf by currents create a plankton bloom. That feast continues through mid-September.

Scientists have documented that populations on the Meso-American Reef, stretching from Honduras up to Yucatán, travel into the northern Gulf of Mexico. In 2008, Rachel Graham, now executive director of Mar Alliance in Belize, tagged a whale shark off the Yucatán Peninsula that triggered a detector in August 2009 at Bright Bank in the Gulf, roughly

100 miles from the coasts of Texas and Louisiana. Graham has tracked individuals tagged on the Meso-American Reef to waters off South Padre Island, Texas, as well.

Given this tagging evidence and observation of whale sharks swimming in both the northern and southern Gulf of Mexico and Caribbean from June to September, scientists suspect that individuals move back and forth between these areas, depending on the opportunity to feed. Graham reports that the sharks can easily travel about six miles per day. Whale sharks also frequent waters off Western Australia and eastern Africa in season.

Threats to Whale Sharks

The IUCN's Red List of Threatened Species ranks whale sharks as Endangered (www.iucnredlist.org/details/19488/0). Whale sharks are listed in CITES Appendix II. The species is considered Threatened in Mexico, and in the United States it is protected from being taken for fishing under the Magnuson-Stevens Fishery Conservation and Management Act.

The major threats to whale sharks include international trade and targeting by directed fisheries. Their low numbers and predictable movements make them particularly vulnerable, and, like many other types of sharks, whale sharks have suffered high human predation. Currently, whale sharks enjoy protection from fishing in Mexico, the Philippines, Australia, and the United States, and, according to Graham, the Gulf of Mexico and Caribbean populations remain in pretty good shape so far.

Whale sharks also face threats from ocean pollution and ship traffic. The aggregations of whale sharks sometimes occur in shipping lanes, and feeding at the surface exposes them to high risk of ship strikes.

Improper tourism practices also pose a threat. Tourist activities occur at key feeding sites, and divers and snorkelers have reported that when they move in front of an individual, it often dives, disrupting its feeding. People disturbing them at key feeding sites affects the animals' fitness and ultimately their survival.

Yucatán fishermen were the first to notice the nearby whale shark aggregations and to start taking tourists out to see them. Out of concern for how this might affect the animals, the World Wildlife Fund asked local outfitter Kenneth Johnson of EcoColors to work with Graham and others to develop rules that would help minimize any harm this tourism might cause.

Graham had already done this in Belize. Trained guides there are primarily locals who have a personal stake in following guidelines that protect the shark population and, therefore, their livelihoods. This approach to tourism management makes it possible to continue giving people a chance to interact with these large animals in their natural environment, something not possible anywhere else on earth.

Seeing Whale Sharks in Mexico

Unlike charismatic species that have spawned many tourist operations, such as dolphins and sea turtles, whale sharks do not come to shore or follow your boat. You have to go where they are.

Massive summer plankton blooms attract filter-feeding whale sharks to waters off the Yucatán Peninsula where the Caribbean Sea meets the Gulf of Mexico. In 2009, Mexico designated 145,988 acres of water surface as the Reserva de la Biosfera Tiburón Ballena, off the northern coast of Quintana Roo. Five-day trips to Isla Mujeres with Reefs to Rockies include snorkeling with the big, spotted sharks, which locals call dominos.

Three days of the trip include morning whale shark tours, traveling by boat 25 miles off the coast to swim and snorkel with whale sharks feeding on plankton in the deep water. The huge figures seem to materialize out of the blue, each a Mack truck of a fish in perpetual first gear with a flat, wide mouth for a grill. Ghostly gray and covered in white spots, the animals motor along, swinging massive tails and curving caudal fins.

Afternoons are free to explore the island. Trip cost includes a donation on behalf of each participant to ECOCEAN, which maintains a whale shark photo-identification library, a collection of images from whale

Whale shark in the Gulf of Mexico
Credit: Cancun Convention and Visitors Bureau

shark encounters that marine biologists use to learn more about the elusive animals.

If you are already in the area, local outfitter EcoColors Tours operates day excursions from Cancún, Playa del Carmen, and Tulum to the reserve. Spotting at least one of the animals is practically guaranteed in season, and they often come quite close to the boats and snorkelers. This tour includes lunch on the beach and return to your hotel between 2:00 and 4:00 p.m.

Trips to see whale sharks also depart from Isla Holbox, about two hours by car and a 30-minute boat ride from Cancún. Once on the island, everything is within easy walking distance. V. I. P. Holbox Experience on the island offers guided day tours to swim with whale sharks. These start with a briefing and light breakfast followed by a one- to two-hour boat ride to find where the whale sharks are feeding that day. Typically, you will be swimming in waters that are green and murky due to the plankton bloom that draws in the whale sharks. On the return trip, the boat stops at Cabo Catoche for snorkeling with other marine life such as sea turtles, nurse sharks, and reef fish, and at Santa Paula for fresh ceviche on the beach.

Travel tips Remember never to touch the whale sharks, swim in front of them, or in any way interfere with their feeding. Speak up if a boat driver or guide disregards proper practices for whale shark encounters —they usually do so in an effort to please clients, so this feedback is especially important.

Seeing Whale Sharks in Belize

Dive boats depart Placencia, Belize, and travel over miles of rolling blue water, past green cayes like a string of stepping-stones, some with brightly colored houses and neat docks, but most empty and inviting. At the end of the roughly 75-minute ride, boats stop to pay rangers an entry fee to Gladden Spit protected area. The rangers work for Southern Environmental Association Belize, an organization enforcing limits on the number of boats and people and the required certification for guides who bring them here. With no land in sight, they work out of a small boat.

Shortly after the full moons in spring, some 26 different fish species spawn en masse at Gladden Spit, which attracts filter-feeding whale sharks. They seem to especially favor the spawn of Cubera snapper.

Whale sharks gathering in large groups to feed make an unforgettable sight, and diving rather than snorkeling means spending more time observing the animals. But this trip is not for the faint of heart. The dive site lies outside Belize's protective barrier reef, and what feels like the entire Caribbean fetches up here, huge swells rearing the boat high into the air and sending plumes of white spray reaching the top deck when it crashes back down. At the recreational diving limit of 100 feet, the reef lies another 30 feet or so below, and beyond, the view drops off into endless blue. Common sights include schools of swirling fish, moon jellies, and dolphins.

Travel Information

Reefs to Rockies, Isla Mujeres, Mexico: Tours mid-July to mid-August, (303) 860-6045, http://reefstorockies.com/destinations/north-america-2/mexico/

EcoColors Tours, Cancun, Mexico: Snorkel tours June–September, https://www.ecotravelmexico.com

V. I. P. Holbox Experience, Isla Holbox, Mexico: Snorkel tours mid-May to mid-September, www.vipholbox.com

Southern Environmental Association (SEA) Belize, Placencia, Belize: March–April, http://seabelize.org/whale-shark/

Travel tips Stormy weather and rough seas are a possibility. Check the US State Department website for travel alerts and the CDC website for recommended precautions against mosquito-borne illnesses.

Indo-Pacific and Asia

Bengal tiger, Tadoba-Andhari Tiger Reserve, India
Credit: Harshawardhan Dhanwatey

Bengal Tiger

Panthera tigris tigris

Kanha National Park and Tiger Reserve, India

NATURAL HABITAT ADVENTURES AND WORLD WILDLIFE FUND

The largest member of the cat family, tigers reach lengths of 10 feet and weigh between 250 and 550 pounds. Their famously beautiful coats range from yellow to light orange in color, with stripes of dark brown to black, white bellies, and orange tails with black rings. These colors and patterns serve as camouflage for tigers while resting or hunting; no two have exactly the same stripe pattern. White tigers represent a variation in color of the Bengal tiger and can be pure white or have black stripes.

Bengal tigers arrived on the Indian subcontinent approximately 12,000 years ago. A century ago, as many as 50,000 to 80,000 of the big cats roamed India alone. Today, the Bengal tiger occurs mostly in India —a 2010 survey estimated a population of 1,706—with small numbers in Nepal, Bhutan, and Bangladesh for a total population of fewer than 2,500.

Scientists generally recognize eight subspecies of tigers (*P. tigris*): Bengal, Indo-Chinese, South China, Amur, Sumatran, Bali, Javan, and Caspian. The latter three—found near the Caspian Sea in Turkey, in Iran, and on Bali and Java islands—have already become extinct.

Tigers live in a variety of habitats, from Russia's far eastern temperate forests to mangrove swamps of the Sunderbans of Bangladesh and western India, and dry and wet deciduous forests, grasslands, and marshes of India and Indonesia.

Bengal tigers live alone, scent-marking their large territories to keep rivals away. They hunt at night, traveling long distances to take buffalo, deer, wild pigs, and other large mammals, creeping in close to attack with one quick, fatal pounce. One tiger can eat as much as 60 pounds in one night but typically eats less. Tigers usually avoid humans. A few have become man-eaters, most likely because they are sick and unable to hunt normally or because traditional prey has vanished in their territory.

Females have litters of two to six cubs, and males provide little or no help raising them. Cubs start to hunt at about 18 months of age and remain with their mothers for two to three years before dispersing to find their own territory. They live 8 to 10 years in the wild. A tiger's roar

Bengal tigers, Tadoba-Andhari Tiger Reserve, India
Credit: Harshawardhan Dhanwatey

can be heard for distances up to two miles away, in part because tigers produce low-frequency sounds.

Threats to Bengal Tigers

All tiger subspecies are listed as Endangered under the ESA, which prohibits import into the country of tiger parts and products, except under certain conditions. Bengal tigers also are listed as IUCN Endangered and Protected in CITES Appendix I (www.iucnredlist.org/details/136899/0).

The increasing human population has caused major loss of tiger habitat, and what remains is fragmented by agriculture and forest clearing for development and roads networks. Tigers must crowd into small and scattered patches of habitat. Tigers face significant decline in their natural prey, deer and antelopes, due to poaching for meat and trade and competition with livestock for food. Removal of wood for fires causes degradation of their habitat. These two threats increasingly bring tigers into conflict with humans and have resulted in tigers attacking domestic animals and even, occasionally, people. People often kill tigers in retaliation.

Tiger populations were decimated by poaching and trade before an international ban in 1993. Illegal demand remains high for tiger as trophies, skins, and decorative items and for body parts used in Chinese folk medicine. Practitioners of this folk medicine believe tiger parts cure rheumatism, convulsions, typhoid fever, dysentery, and other diseases, and tiger bone can fetch prices as high as $115 dollars per pound for such uses. Poaching to fuel this international illegal trade represents the most significant, immediate threat to the population.

The World Wildlife Fund (WWF) and TRAFFIC, a wildlife trade-monitoring network, work to stop black-market trade in tiger products and parts in Asia by funding antipoaching patrols and supporting intelligence networks in strategic locations. WWF also supports the South Asia Wildlife Enforcement Network (SAWEN), which regional governments use to combine information and resources, including early-warning systems, advocating for effective legislation, and improving law enforcement.

Losing Earth's Large Mammals

Since the dawn of modern man, humans have caused the decline and extinction of a growing list of animals. Large-bodied mammals such as tigers typically face a higher risk of extinction than smaller ones, and today, most mammalian megafauna—typically those 90 pounds and larger—face serious population declines. A group of 43 wildlife experts from around the world recently published a paper reporting that 59 percent of the world's largest carnivores and 60 percent of the largest herbivores are classified as Threatened with extinction on the IUCN Red List. The problem is especially acute in Sub-Saharan Africa and Southeast Asia, places that have the greatest diversity of these megafauna—including tigers.

Many of these animals, including gorillas, rhinos, and big cats, may disappear just as science discovers their essential ecological roles. Many of them function as keystone species and ecological engineers, generating strong cascading effects through entire ecosystems. For example, read about the trophic or food-chain cascade dependent on wolves in the "North America" section. These animals tend to drive ecotourism activities as well, with all its associated benefits to local economies.

The scientists note that ongoing and escalating habitat loss, persecution, and exploitation bear the blame for this impending disaster. Large mammals are particularly vulnerable to these threats given their need for large area and low density (particularly for carnivores) and their low reproductive rates.

Humans continue to kill these large mammals for meat, body parts for traditional medicine, and ornaments or because of actual or perceived threats to humans, their crops, or livestock. Without swift, sustained action, many of these species may vanish forever. Already, we have lost the western black rhinoceros and Vietnamese subspecies of the Javan rhinoceros; next on the list could be the kouprey, last seen in 1988, and the northern white rhinoceros, with only two individuals remaining. Sumatran rhinos went extinct in the wild in Malaysia, and only a single group of 58 Javan rhinos remains. Bactrian camel and African wild ass, lions, African wild dogs, and cheetahs could disappear as well.

The authors stress that we need a comprehensive global strategy for conserving these large mammals and the political will to restore or reintroduce them. The problem, they add, has two parts: "a need to further and more effectively implement, expand, and refine current interventions at relevant scales and a need for large-scale policy shifts and global increases in funding for conservation to alter the framework and ways in which people interact with wildlife." Funding for this work must be increased by at least an order of magnitude.

"We must not go quietly into this impoverished future," they write. "Rather, we believe it is our collective responsibility as scientists who study megafauna to act to prevent their decline. We therefore present a call to the broader international community to join together in conserving the remaining terrestrial megafauna."

Nations around the world must unite to provide social, political, and financial commitments. Travelers can take the lead in demanding these commitments before it is too late.*

Seeing Tigers in India

Natural Habitat Adventures offers several tour itineraries to see tigers. A 12-day Grand India Wildlife Adventure includes visiting 444-square-mile Bandhavgarh National Park and Tiger Reserve, known for one of India's highest concentrations of the endangered cat. Forest, thickets of bamboo, and expansive grasslands cover the park's hilly terrain, supporting rich biodiversity that includes 37 mammal species, such as leopard, jungle cat, civet, wild boar, sambar, spotted deer, muntjac (barking deer), sloth, and Asiatic jackal. The park also houses some 250 bird species, 70 different butterflies, and various reptiles.

* William J. Rippel et al., "Saving the World's Terrestrial Megafauna," *BioScience* 66, no. 10 July 27, 2016, bioscience.oxfordjournals.org/content/early/2016/07/25/biosci.biw092.full.

For two and a half days, the group explores the park on morning and afternoon wildlife drives in open 4 x 4 safari trucks. The trip then moves on to Kanha National Park and Tiger Reserve in central India's Satpura Hills. These 750 square miles sport forests, grassy meadows, and ravines and inspired Rudyard Kipling's famous novel *The Jungle Book*. The park, established in 1955, and reserve, created in 1974, also saved the rare, hard-ground swamp deer from near extinction. Here, the tour spends two full days searching for Bengal tigers and other wildlife on excursions in open 4 x 4 vehicles. This area's ideal habitat for tigers and their prey offers some of India's best tiger viewing.

Guests may also see chowsingha (four-horned antelopes), common langurs, gaurs (the world's largest wild oxen), rhesus monkeys, and leopards.

"We focus on getting people away from hordes of tourists and into places they can have authentic encounters that are less intrusive on the animal," says Natural Habitat's Wendy Redal. "Bandhavgarh has the highest concentration of tigers and fewer people, and we spend three days there exploring and have a really good chance of encountering tigers. In Kanha, we go on jeep safaris with our expert naturalist and local guides, who are very good at tracking tigers. Tigers are hard to see; they have amazing camouflage and prefer to stay hidden," she adds. "It is not like seeing lions out on the Serengeti; it takes some effort. When you do see them, it is a real reward."

Placing only two people per vehicle ensures the best wildlife-watching experience possible. "Our small groups not only guarantee more personal, close-up wildlife encounters but also ensure a lower impact on these special places," says Redal.

Natural Habitat also offers a seven-day tiger and wildlife photo safari in India's Ranthambore National Park in eastern Rajasthan, legendary tiger country. Hot weather means few visitors and, because tigers must come to water holes at least twice a day, a higher chance of seeing them.

Both tours use the services of eco-lodges near the parks. Redal notes that tours also directly help protect tigers. In 2014 in India, the most recent tiger population count rose 30 percent from four years earlier, and responsible nature tourism contributed to that rise. The economic contribution of visitors benefits communities around the tiger reserves and provides an incentive for local people to protect these wild creatures. India is the only country where tiger numbers have risen, and its wildlife tourism shares the credit for that success.

Carbon Offsets for Travelers

Worldwide, travel-related activities account for up to 14 percent of greenhouse gas emissions. A portion of every plane flight emits an average of nearly a ton of greenhouse gases. Natural Habitat offsets 100 percent of carbon emissions from its trips in partnership with nonprofit Sustainable Travel International, which calculates the amount of carbon emissions from specific travel activities. In fact, in 2007, Natural Habitat became the world's first carbon-neutral travel company, and in 2014, it offset more than 3,096 metric tons of carbon dioxide for its travelers.

Examples of carbon reduction projects include reforestation of native tree species, installation of solar panels, construction of wind turbines, and providing zero-energy water purifiers to replace burning of nonrenewable biomass to boil water for drinking.

"On our website, you can find carbon offset projects we are involved with," says Redal. "Look under a tab that says why travel with us, the sustainability and conservation tab. One example, Bull Run in Belize, is an area where we are preventing forest being cleared for coffee growing. Another provides water filters that keep people from having to cut nonrenewable biomass to boil water."

Travel Information

Natural Habitat/World Wildlife Fund: (800) 543-8917, http://nathab .com/asia-adventure-travel/

Giant panda in a research and conservation facility in China
Credit: Brad Josephs

Giant Panda

Ailuropoda melanoleuca

Sichuan, China

NATURAL HABITAT ADVENTURES

Mention endangered animals and many people immediately think of pandas. This species became inextricably linked with conservation when the World Wildlife Fund—the first international conservation organization invited by the Chinese government to work in that country—adopted the giant panda as its logo.

Giant pandas live only in China, in six isolated mountain ranges in the Gansu, Shaanxi, and Sichuan Provinces. Also known as bamboo bear, or *daxiongmao*, which means "large bear cat" in Chinese, its scientific name means "black-and-white cat-footed animal."

Adult pandas can grow to heights greater than 4 feet and weigh between 220 and 330 pounds. Despite their size, pandas easily climb trees.

Pandas live in temperate montane forests at altitudes of 5,000 to 10,000 feet, where they can find dense stands of bamboo, their primary food. Pandas eat more than 60 species of the plant but prefer 35 of them in particular, the type varying with season and elevation. An adult must eat from 26 to 84 pounds of bamboo daily and spends more than half of its time doing so. Pandas have enlarged wrist bones that act almost as opposable thumbs, which helps them pull off and eat bamboo shoots.

These bears do not hibernate but often will move to lower elevations in winter and take shelter in hollow trees, rock crevices, and caves. Successful reproduction of pandas in captivity has proved quite difficult, but several studies indicate that in the wild, panda reproductive rates compare to those of some other species of bears. Even captive populations in China now reproduce successfully.

These bears usually remain solitary except during mating season from March to May. Females may mate with multiple males. They typically give birth in rock dens or hollow trees, August to September, and while a mother may have one or two cubs, she raises only one. Newborn pandas are tiny, small enough to fit in the palm of a person's hand.

As pandas roam bamboo forests, they spread seeds that lead to growth of vegetation. A wide range of other wildlife calls the Yangtze Basin forests home, including dwarf blue sheep, multicolored pheasants, and other endangered species such as the golden monkey, takin, and crested ibis.

Goodwill Ambassadors

China has given or loaned giant pandas to zoos around the world as symbols of friendship. Two of these, Ling-Ling and Hsing-Hsing, went to the National Zoo in Washington, DC, in the 1970s. These on-loan giant pandas are part of robust scientific conservation programs supporting efforts in China to enhance long-term survival of the species. The loans are coordinated through the Association of Zoos and Aquarium's (AZA) Giant Panda Species Survival Plan (SSP), and participating institutions hold ESA and CITES permits.

Threats to Pandas

US FWS listed the giant panda as an Endangered species under the ESA in 1984. CITES included it under Appendix I. The IUCN Red List previously listed it as Endangered but changed that status to Vulnerable in September 2016 (www.iucnredlist.org/details/712/0). The population rose 17 percent from 2004 to 2014, when a nationwide census counted 1,864 giant pandas in the wild in China.

Giant pandas in a research and conservation facility in China
Credit: Brad Josephs

Significant change in climate, human cultivation of low and flat areas for thousands of years, and hunting have combined to drastically shrink the giant panda's original range. That range once included most of southern and eastern China, and fossils indicate that pandas even lived southward into northern Myanmar, north into Vietnam, and nearly to Beijing. The pygmy giant panda (*A. microta*), a relative of giant pandas once found in this area, went extinct.

Logging and clearing land for farming left small and isolated populations of pandas confined to high ridges in six mountain ranges. Agricultural development separates these mountain ranges, and, even within them, cleared lands and forest without bamboo understory separate the remaining fragments of bamboo forest. Their small population and limited range make these animals particularly vulnerable.

The panda's reliance on bamboo for food also presents a problem; bamboo is subject to periodic, large-scale flowering and die-off. Pandas could move from an area experiencing die-off to one with healthy bamboo before humans encroached so significantly on their habitat. Now it is more difficult for them to find patches of healthy bamboo or to move to other areas where they could feed on other species of bamboo.

While a significant problem in the past, poaching has diminished as markets for panda skins virtually disappeared and penalties became more severe. Traditional Chinese medicine does not use panda parts, but giant pandas sometimes die in snares set for other species. While China has established more than 50 panda reserves, they protect only about 60 percent of the population.

Seeing Pandas in China

Natural Habitat Adventures offers a 12-day, all-inclusive trip, On the Wild Side of China Photo Adventure. It explores wilderness that is home to rare golden monkeys, shaggy takins, Asiatic black bears, and the endangered giant panda. The outfitter has received special permits allowing its tours to visit one of China's most remote nature reserves and the places where wild pandas live and breed. While the bears' numbers are few and their nature elusive, this provides travelers with one of the best chances to see and photograph them. Group size is limited to 12, and expedition leaders are naturalists and expert nature and wildlife photographers, happy to provide tips and techniques. A Chinese tour escort and local guides also join the trip to talk about both historic and contemporary Chinese culture.

The tour starts in Chengdu, capital of Sichuan Province, and travels to nearby Dujiangyan Panda Valley, a research and breeding base with a focus on education and conservation. Panda Valley habituates pandas for release into the wild. The next day includes a visit to the Research Base of Giant Panda Breeding, a research and educational tourism center, where some 100 pandas live in a human-made environment built to resemble their natural habitat as closely as possible.

The following day includes a scenic drive into the Minshan Mountains, northward along the Fu River to a chain of nature reserves outside the Gansu Muslim village of Qing Xi. The next two days are spent exploring a 100,000-acre, densely forested sanctuary and national reserve, rated by WWF as a top-tier global biodiversity hotspot with some of the world's most endangered wildlife, including at least 60 giant pandas. While sighting one of them is a rare treat, tour participants more easily see some of the 150 species of birds, Tibetan and rhesus macaques, golden and Sichuan takins, musk deer, muntjacs, serows, wild boar, blue sheep, and, on occasion, endangered moon bears and red pandas. Leopards, civets, and hog-nosed badgers may appear on night drives and walks.

The group travels on to Jiuzhai Valley on the edge of the Tibetan Plateau for two days in Jiuzhiagou National Park, a UNESCO World Heritage Site and UN Biosphere Reserve deep in the Minshan Mountains. This area offers bird and wildlife watching in a landscape of steep peaks, ravines, forest, meadows, marshes, lakes, and waterfalls.

The trip wraps up with a visit to a third panda base, the research center at Dujiangyan. Its work includes disease control and prevention, rescue and rehabilitation of wild pandas that are sick or injured, and care for senior and disabled pandas.

Natural Habitat Adventures is a carbon-neutral travel company and focuses on sustainable practices both at home and throughout its operations abroad.

Symbol of Conservation

Inspiration for the WWF panda logo came from Chi-Chi, a giant panda at the London Zoo, in 1961, the year the organization began. WWF founders wanted a strong, recognizable symbol unfettered by language barriers and decided that this large, furry animal and its notable black-patched eyes fit the bill. British environmentalist and artist Gerald

Watterson created initial sketches, and conservationist and painter Sir Peter Scott, one of the organization's founders, used them to draw the first logo. While the logo evolved over time, the distinctive features of a panda came to serve as a universal symbol for conservation.

Working with the Chinese National Conservation Program, WWF advocates for increased protected habitat; green corridors created to connect isolated populations; patrols to combat poaching, illegal logging and encroachment; local capacity building for reserve management; and ongoing research and monitoring. Panda reserves currently take in more than 3.8 million acres of forest.

Travel Information

Natural Habitat Adventures: (800) 543-8917, https://www.nathab
.com/asia-adventure-travel/wild-ancient-china-photo-tour/

Travel tips Tours reach high altitudes and involve strenuous hikes. Check the CDC website for the latest on avian flu and precautions to take against this virus. Some panda reserves are open to daily visitors.

Coral species on the Great Barrier Reef

Credit: Farbenfrohe Wunderwelt

Great Barrier Reef, Reef-Building Corals

Australia

HERON ISLAND RESORT

Coral reefs have been called the Manhattan of the ocean—while they may not look it, coral reefs are living structures made up of many tiny individual animals and teeming with all sorts of other marine creatures. Reefs often stretch for many miles and may reach from near the surface of the sea to far below it.

There are thousands of species of coral, hundreds of them the hard corals that build reefs. Soft corals, found in both tropical and cold oceans, do not produce reefs. Individual hard coral animals, called polyps, have soft, tubular bodies and a ring of tentacles on top. Each individual polyp creates an external skeleton around its base made of calcium carbonate. Thousands of polyps connected together by a thin layer of tissue make up a coral colony. Corals can grow in one of two ways: polyps can lift off their base and secrete a new skeleton by adding layers of calcium, or individual polyps can reproduce. Reefs form from the growth of thousands or more of these coral colonies.

Corals reproduce both sexually and asexually. Asexual reproduction involves a polyp budding or splitting in two, then each of those two polyps dividing, and so on, for the rest of their lives. All of these polyps are genetically identical. Sexual reproduction by definition mixes genetic material from different polyps. About three-quarters of reef-building coral species reproduce through broadcast spawning, which means males and females simultaneously release large quantities of sperm and eggs into the water. These float to the surface where sperm fertilize eggs and form free-floating larvae.

All members of a specific coral species must spawn at the same time, of course, for their eggs and sperm to find each other. Scientists do not know exactly how corals do this, but the cues for spawning involve some combination of the phase of the moon, solar cycle, ocean temperature, and cues from chemical composition of the water and length of daylight. Spawning occurs at different times on different reefs. At the Flower Garden Banks National Marine Sanctuary in the Gulf of Mexico, for example, mass spawning occurs in August 7 to 10 days after the full moon. Scientists are able to predict the time individual species will spawn almost to the minute. These species spawn one after the other in the same order each time. Free-floating coral larvae drift on ocean currents for up to two weeks before settling to the bottom as polyps. Sexual reproduction, therefore, helps create completely new colonies and reefs.

In the other form of sexual reproduction, brooding, males release sperm that are captured from the water by female polyps. Eggs are fertilized inside the females and larvae released. These larvae settle to the bottom relatively soon so do not travel as far from their parent colony as those from broadcast spawning.

Growth rates of coral reefs vary, with some massive corals growing less than an inch per year while branching corals can grow as much as four inches per year. A sizable reef may take thousands of years to form, and barrier reefs and atolls form over hundreds of thousands to millions of years. Reef-building corals grow best in water that is clear enough to allow sunlight to penetrate, at temperatures between 73 and 84 degrees, and salinity of 32 to 42 parts per thousand. These conditions are found primarily in tropical or subtropical waters, or between latitudes 30 degrees north and 30 degrees south, and down to about 230 feet, in what is known as the euphotic or light-penetration zone of the ocean.

Corals need light because they have algae, or zooxanthellae, living within the tissues of polyps. This symbiotic relationship works well for both, with coral providing the algae a home and the algae in turn provid-

Corals and reef fish on the Great Barrier Reef
Credit: Kyle Taylor, USFWS

ing coral polyps with 80 percent of their food through photosynthesis, using sunlight.

If the open ocean resembles a desert, coral reefs function like oases in that desert, providing food and shelter for marine life. According to the Global Coral Bleaching consortium, while coral reefs account for only 0.1 percent of the world's ocean floor, some 25 percent of all marine species rely on them. This includes juvenile fish that seek shelter in reefs until they grow large enough to survive in the open ocean. This 25 percent of species supports the livelihoods of more than 500 million people and has an economic value of $1 trillion. The US National Oceanic and Atmospheric Administration (NOAA) estimates that US fisheries from coral reefs have an annual economic value of more than $100 million. According to the Climate Council of Australia, in 2011–12, the Great Barrier Reef represented a value-added economic contribution to the Australian economy of $5.7 billion and supported 69,000 jobs. Other important services provided by coral reefs include protecting shorelines from storm surge and attracting tourism dollars to local economies.

Threats to Coral Reefs

The ESA lists 22 coral species as Threatened and 3—*Cantharellus noumeae, Siderastrea glynni*, and *Tubastraea floreana*—as Endangered. Threatened species include elkhorn, staghorn, and star corals (www.nmfs .noaa.gov/pr/species/invertebrates/corals.htm). Nearly 30 percent of the world's reef-building corals—which total 845 species—appear as Threatened on the IUCN Red List, with an additional 20 percent considered Near Threatened. The IUCN considers staghorn coral (*Acropora cervicornis*) and elkhorn coral (*A. palmata*) as Critically Endangered. The IUCN notes that reef-building corals have not been reassessed since 2009 (cmsdata.iucn.org/downloads/resilience_assessment_final.pdf); there are plans to do so by 2020, but the funding for this work is not yet secured (iucn.org/content/corals-%E2%80%93-ecosystem-risk). All coral species are listed in CITES Appendix II, including all stony, blue, organ pipe, and fire corals. Black, pink, and red corals, also known as precious corals, face high demand for use in jewelry and carvings (fws .gov/international/animals/coral.html).

Threats to coral reefs include overfishing, dredging, coastal development, pollution (including sediment and agricultural runoff), disease, predation, the aquarium trade, boat and anchor strikes and collisions, marine debris, and invasive species. Climate change, however, currently represents the most serious threat to corals. An IUCN study found 566 of 799 warm-water, reef-building coral species especially susceptible to the effects of climate change. One of the major effects is rising water temperatures. For more than 50 years, global average temperatures have increased significantly. and the planet's 10 warmest years have been recorded since 1998. The oceans absorb 93 percent of this increasing heat in the atmosphere, which has increased the surface temperatures of ocean waters by one degree Fahrenheit in that same 50 years. Corals have not been able to adapt to the rapid rise in temperatures overall or extended periods of unusually high temperatures.

Water temperatures higher than normal for corals cause a phenomenon known as bleaching. When stressed, such as by higher-than-normal temperatures, corals force out their symbiotic algae. This exposes their white calcium carbonate skeletons and produces a "bleached" look. While the coral animal remains alive, it now takes in only 20 percent of the food it needs. If water temperatures return to normal quickly enough and remain there long enough, polyps can then again take in algae and recover. Otherwise, the polyps eventually die. Different species of algae grow over their skeletons, preventing new coral polyps from landing to replenish the reef. A bleached reef shifts from primarily coral to primarily algae, resulting in much less biodiversity and providing less habitat for fish and other organisms.

Scientists see this happening throughout the world's oceans. A mass coral bleaching event affects an entire reef system, not just a few individual corals. Scientists recorded the first such event in 1979, as well as 60 local bleaching events between 1979 and 1990. A global coral bleaching event involves tropical ocean basins in the Atlantic, Pacific, and Indian Oceans; the first of these occurred in 1998, killing at least 15 percent of global reefs. A second global event happened in 2010. The third and longest-lasting global event so far started in 2014 and continued worldwide through June 2017. By the end of 2016, bleaching had affected more than 42 percent of the world's reefs across the Southern Hemisphere, the Caribbean, Atlantic, and Pacific.

Climate change clearly plays a huge role in this latest global bleaching event, says Mark Eakin, coordinator of the NOAA Coral Reef Watch. This program uses satellites to collect data on environmental conditions, including sea-surface temperatures, to identify corals at risk of bleaching. Coral Reef Watch scientists also visually monitor reefs to determine coral health.

Particularly widespread bleaching occurred in the Southern Hemisphere during the 2015–16 summer season. Jodie Rummer, senior research fellow at the ARC Centre of Excellence for Coral Reef Studies at Australia's James Cook University, attributes that to the combination of an early El Niño, an extended period of hot summer days, and lower-than-normal tides, a sort of perfect storm of conditions. El Niño, a periodic weather phenomenon throughout the tropical Pacific, creates warmer-than-usual ocean temperatures in an area from the central to eastern Equatorial Pacific, affecting weather patterns around the globe. Fishermen first noticed this phenomenon and named it El Niño because it typically began around Christmas.

An April 2017 report from the Climate Council of Australia reported bleaching in 2016 on 91 percent of individual reefs in the Great Barrier Reef—four times worse than in the 2002 and 1998 events. Bleaching hit northernmost reefs the hardest, with the council also reporting loss of 67 percent of coral cover on the Great Barrier Reef north of Port Douglas. Preliminary surveys in early 2017 indicated widespread bleaching under way yet again. This bleaching event ranks as the worst ever seen on the Great Barrier Reef (so far).

Record-breaking bleaching events also occurred on reefs of the Hawaiian Islands, American Samoa, Guam, the Commonwealth of the Northern Mariana Islands, and Florida. Globally, severe bleaching hit reefs across the Pacific, Caribbean, and Indian Oceans. Coral Reef Watch predicted widespread bleaching and mortality in the Cook Islands, American Samoa, and Kiribati from April to July in 2017.

According to the Nature Conservancy's Reef Resilience project, scientists predict that by the 2050s, 95 percent of the world's coral reefs face potential bleaching due to high thermal stress. The long-term effects of bleaching reverberate far beyond the loss of corals. Fish and other animals depend on reefs for food or shelter and will move away when reefs die, or these animals die themselves, which ripples up the food chain. Even birds may move on, causing a chain reaction in island ecosystems, where bird droppings often provide an important source of nourishment for plants.

Loss of corals affects people who rely on the fish and other creatures that live on reefs for food. The fisheries and tourism industries also suffer, creating economic hardship in areas that depend on these industries. Without the protection afforded by reefs, coastal areas experience increased erosion and damage from storm surges—further exacerbated by increased severity of storms due to climate change.

How You Can Help

The healthier a coral reef, the better it is able to recover from bleaching, so it helps reduce the other causes of stress noted earlier. Scientists have begun work to increase the overall health of coral reefs. The Nature Conservancy offers workshops and training on resilience for reef managers. Researchers are working to identify coral species that have higher tolerance to increasing water temperatures and testing ways to introduce them in areas at risk of bleaching. Ultimately, however, climate change must be addressed. A report from the Climate Council of Australia states that "the future of coral reefs depends on how much and how fast we reduce greenhouse gas emissions now, and in the coming years and decades. Global emissions must be trending downwards by 2020 at the latest."

For individuals, the number-one priority is reducing their carbon footprint, according to Eakin. Individuals also can affect local stressors such as overfishing and land use practices that allow soil and nutrients to wash into the ocean. Tourists, especially those who snorkel or scuba dive on and around coral reefs, can choose outfitters that follow good environment practices, such as anchoring away from reefs or using mooring buoys.

No one should ever touch coral with their hands, fins, or other gear.

Research shows that sunscreen containing oxybenzone (benzophenone-3) or similar compounds harms corals. More than 3,500 sunscreen products around the world contain oxybenzone, researchers report. An individual might use between two to four ounces of sunblock during a day at the beach, an amount multiplied by the number of people using sunscreen and swimming in the ocean during a summer. Researchers even found oxybenzone pollution on reefs as much as 20 miles from shore. Furthermore, the chemical showed toxicity effect in concentrations as low as 62 parts per trillion—or a drop of water in more than six Olympic-sized swimming pools. Look for sunscreens without this ingredient, such as those using only zinc oxide or titanium dioxide, or use sun-blocking clothing.

Finally, people can act as citizen-scientists and contribute to collection of global coral data. Bleach Patrol, an app developed by Columbia University and the World Surfing League, makes it possible for anyone to report bleached or healthy reefs anywhere in the world at any time. The resulting data set, Eakin says, helps scientists document the geographic extent and patterns of bleaching, showing them when and where corals are bleaching or healthy.

Seeing Coral on the Great Barrier Reef

The Great Barrier Reef consists of some 3,000 individual reefs that stretch more than 1,400 miles. It represents the largest structure ever created by living organisms, billions and billions of coral polyps from more than 350 different species. Parts of it are 20 million years old, and the colorful reefs visible today are about 10,000 years old. It provides habitat for more than 1,500 species of fish as well as crustaceans, starfish, sea turtles, and more.

Heron Island, a natural coral cay and national park 55 miles off the coast of Queensland within the Great Barrier Reef, houses a resort operated by a concessionaire, Delaware North Companies Parks and Resorts. The island is accessible by a regular ferry or scheduled seaplane from Gladstone, between Brisbane and Cairns on Australia's northeastern coast.

Endangered green and loggerhead sea turtles nest on the island's broad, sandy beaches from November through March. Heron Island partners with the Sea Turtle Foundation to protect and conserve these marine reptiles, and guests may make an optional $10AUS donation to the foundation on their room bill. Heron Island also serves as a breeding and nesting sanctuary for a variety of birds, including black noddy terns, wedgetail shearwaters, and eastern reef egrets. Certain months bring up to 100,000 birds to the tiny island. The resort has cottages that sleep two, family cottages sleeping up to four, Reef Rooms with beach views for three and five people, and suites. All rooms include daily breakfast at the on-site restaurant.

The clear, blue waters around Heron Island contain some 60 percent of the 1,500 species of fish and 72 percent of coral species of the Great Barrier Reef. Manta rays and sharks are common sights. Visitors can book boat excursions to snorkel and scuba dive on the reefs. The island sits directly on the reef, with some 20 diving sites within a 5- to 15-minute boat ride, all within the marine national park. The resort caters to all levels of divers, with equipment, platform-style dive boats, experienced dive masters, and even scuba lessons.

Shallow reef depths make for excellent snorkeling right from the shore as well. Water temperatures range from lows of 64 degrees in July (winter in the Southern Hemisphere) to 86 degrees in the summer months of January and February. Humpback whales migrate through the area from May to September, and mass coral spawning occurs in December.

Another option for scuba divers is volunteering with Earthwatch on eight-day expeditions to participate in research on coral reef disease at the James Cook University Orpheus Island Research Station. Activities for volunteer divers include conducting underwater surveys and tagging and photographing diseased coral, to help the project monitor coral health over time. Above the water, volunteers set up and conduct experiments measuring light, temperature, pH, and nutrients of the water. This work helps researchers assess reef recovery from recent cyclones, track seasonal changes, and determine effects of light, temperature, and water quality on disease progression.

Orpheus Island is 6.8 miles long and roughly half a mile wide, and most of it is national park. While at the research station, volunteers stay in the two-story Havana House, which accommodates up to 48 visitors. A recreation area in a separate building has a television, video and CD players, stereo, lounge chairs, games, and kitchens. Earthwatch provides all food during the stay.

Travel Information

Heron Island, Australia: (716) 276-0078 (US); 1800-837-168 (Australia), www.heronisland.com

Earthwatch Expedition, Orpheus Island: (800) 776-0188, http://earthwatch.org/expeditions/recovery-of-the-great-barrier-reef

Travel tips December to February is summer "down under." Temperatures are balmy year-round, ranging from a low of 70 degrees in July to 86 degrees in January. November through March is the monsoon season, with the most rainfall typically occurring in February. Cyclones (hurricanes) can affect Queensland from November to April. Unless you are an Australian or New Zealand citizen, you will need a valid Australian visa to enter the country. Apply online at www.border.gov.au/Trav/Visa-1.

Other Places to See Coral Reefs Responsibly

Flower Garden Banks National Marine Sanctuary, Gulf of Mexico: Fling Charters in Freeport, Texas, operates live-aboard dive trips to these reefs and works closely with sanctuary managers to ensure good practices. The reefs grow on salt domes rising from the seafloor, the shallowest at about 60 feet, so scuba diving is the only way to experience them (https://flow ergarden.noaa.gov/; see "Dive Charters" under the "Visit" tab).

Bonaire: This 12-square-mile island just off the coast of Venezuela has 60-plus shore dive sites in its protected waters. According to the Reef Environmental Education Foundation, which has collected fish surveys from volunteer divers since 1990, Bonaire is its most species-rich survey site in all the Caribbean. A Marine Park tag required to dive here can be purchased at any dive shop (www.tourismbonaire.com/bonaire -dive-sites).

US Virgin Islands: Two-thirds of St. John Island is national park, which has helped protect its marine life. Special permits are required for diving in the park. Low Key Watersports takes divers to Kiddel Bay by appointment. Cane Bay, on the island of St. Croix, and Coki Beach, on the northeastern side of St. Thomas, also offer shore dives (https:// www.visitusvi.com/).

A baby hawksbill turtle makes its way to the ocean in the Solomon Islands

Credit: photo © Tim Calver/The Nature Conservancy

Hawksbill Sea Turtle
Eretmochelys imbricata

Papua New Guinea

WALINDI PLANTATION RESORT

Sea turtles have been around for more than 100 million years. Hawksbills are one of seven sea turtle species found worldwide: others are flatback, green, Kemp's ridley, leatherback, loggerhead, and olive ridley. Although they are air-breathing reptiles, sea turtles spend all their lives at sea, except when females return to the beach on which they were born to nest. A mother sea turtle uses her flippers to dig a deep depression in the sand, where she lays more than 100 eggs before covering them up with sand and returning to the water. The eggs all hatch at the same time, and hatchlings emerge from the nest together—a phenomenon called boiling—and immediately make their way across the beach and into the surf. The temperature in the nest determines the sex of sea turtle hatchlings, with warmer temperatures producing more females and cooler ones more males.

Hawksbills take 20 years or more to reach maturity and begin reproducing. Females then nest every two to three years, laying between three and five egg clutches about 14 days apart during a single nesting season. In Florida and the Caribbean, clutches generally contain around 140 eggs, which incubate for about two months. In most locations around the world, hawksbill nesting occurs between April and November and at night. Hawksbills nest in at least 70 countries, including Mexico, Costa Rica, and remote islands around Australia and in the Indian Ocean. But the number of nests in any given location remains very low.

Adult hawksbills weigh 100 to 200 pounds and have a shell, or carapace, about 30 inches long. The shell bears black and brown markings on a background of amber with overlapping scutes, or scales, and a serrated edge.

Like all sea turtles, hawksbills lack teeth but use the raptorlike jaw from which the species gets its name to eat sponges, which are made of tiny, glasslike needles. Hawksbills play an important role in keeping coral reef ecosystems healthy by controlling sponges that would otherwise outcompete reef-building corals for space. They also consume algae in northern Australia and soft corals in the Great Barrier Reef.

Most sea turtle species are migratory, and individual hawksbills move between a variety of geographic areas and habitats during their lifetimes. Their movements within the marine environment are less understood, but hawksbills may inhabit coastal waters in more than 108 countries.

They live mostly between latitudes of 30 degrees north and south in the Atlantic, Pacific, and Indian Oceans and are found in southern Florida and the Gulf of Mexico, Puerto Rico and the US Virgin Islands, the Lesser Antilles, and along the Central American mainland down to Brazil. Adults spend most of their time around coral reefs but also frequent rocky areas, shallow coastal areas, lagoons or oceanic islands, and narrow creeks and passes, seldom in water deeper than 65 feet. Hatchlings often float in masses of sea plants such as *Sargassum*.

Threats to Sea Turtles

Hawksbill sea turtles qualify as IUCN Critically Endangered and are listed in CITES Appendix I (www.iucnredlist.org/details/8005/0). This species is also listed as Endangered under the ESA. In fact, all species of sea turtles except the flatback are Endangered or Threatened. The IUCN has yet to assess the flatback, found only in Australia, where it is considered Vulnerable by that country and the state of Queensland.

Threats to hawksbills (and many other sea turtles) include human harvest of nesting females for meat, collection of eggs at nesting

Hawksbill sea turtle, Carey de Concha
Credit: Caroline S. Rogers, NOAA

beaches, degradation of nesting and marine habitats, killing of juveniles and adults for food and their shells, and death or injury from commercial fishing lines and nets.

Europeans began fishing hawksbills for meat in the Caribbean in the mid-seventeenth century, with increasing demand throughout the eighteenth century. As fishermen wiped out populations in one area, they moved to another. In 1885, when turtle fishermen could no longer find turtles in the Cayman Islands, they moved to southern Cuba and settled the village of Cocodrilos on the Isle of Pines, operating there for another 100-plus years. Traders in Central America also harvested this sea turtle.

People covet this animal's beautiful shell, often referred to (incorrectly) as tortoiseshell, for jewelry, hair decorations, and other items. Jewelry and other tortoiseshell objects appear in predynastic graves of

Nubian rulers in Egypt and ruins of China's Han Empire. Julius Caesar had warehouses in Alexandria filled with tortoiseshell, and in the early years of the ninth century, Arab caravans carried tortoiseshell along with rhinoceros horn and ivory throughout the Indian Ocean. Around 1700, *bekko*, or tortoiseshell artisans of Japan, appeared at Nagasaki. According to the IUCN assessment, between 1950 and 1992, Japan's *bekko* imports equated to 1,329,044 large turtles; conservatively estimating that 30 percent of those were nesting females, nearly 400,000 adult female hawksbills were killed for the Japanese market in those years. Despite international protections such as CITES, numerous shipments continue to be intercepted by authorities, indicating that some Japanese dealers continue to import shell illegally, and underground trade continues between Japan and Southeast Asia and other destinations.

Up to a quarter million sea turtles die caught on hooks or ensnared in fishing nets each year. The commercial longline fishery puts as many as 1.4 billion hooks into the ocean each year, presenting a significant danger to hawksbill and other sea turtle species. Recreational fishermen often hook or ensnare these and other sea turtles, often juveniles, which tend to forage closer to shorelines.

Beach development destroys or seriously degrades nesting areas, and human activity and lighting also affect nesting females and hatchlings. Sea turtles die or become injured from entanglement in ocean debris, particularly plastic, or from ingesting trash. Nearly all sea turtles that wash ashore dead or dying have plastic in their digestive systems.

Sea-level rise due to climate change contributes to loss of nesting habitat, leaving nesting beaches underwater or more vulnerable to flooding, which drowns hatchlings in their eggs. Hotter temperatures on beaches will skew the sex ratios of hatchlings, and if temperatures rise enough, will kill the hatchlings.

How You Can Help

Make sea turtle-friendly seafood choices, using a reputable seafood guide such as the Monterey Bay Aquarium's Seafood Watch. It offers a smartphone app, a search function on the website, and printable guides specific to different regions ranking choices as Best, Buy (or Acceptable), and Avoid. Ask whether seafood sold at markets and restaurants is sustainable.

Never buy anything made with sea turtle shell. Products still commonly found in many tourist destinations include jewelry, hair combs, and decorative items, often incorrectly called tortoiseshell. The Too Rare to Wear campaign provides more information about trade in sea turtle shell products and how to avoid them on its website: www.tooraretowear.org.

Report nesting or stranded sea turtles to local authorities. In the United States, a stranding network exists that will rescue the animal and take it to a designated facility for rehabilitation and, if possible, release it back into the ocean.

Fish and boat carefully. Cast your line away from visible sea turtles. If you hook a sea turtle, bring it gently close to you and lift it by both front flippers or by its shell, not the hook. Keep it in the shade and call local wildlife authorities so it can be examined for ingested hooks. Never dispose of hooks and line overboard, and recover and recycle monofilament fishing line, which can entangle sea turtles and other marine life.

Slow down your boat to avoid turtles. If you strike a sea turtle, contact local authorities so it can be rescued and treated. Never anchor on coral or seagrass beds.

Reduce your use of disposable plastic. Use refillable water bottles; when traveling to countries where tap water is not safe to drink, fill your bottle with purified water in hotel restaurants or buy one large container and use it to refill your bottle. Use cloth shopping bags, metal forks and spoons, and recyclable paper plates or reusable plastic ones. Avoid using straws when possible, or use metal, glass, or bamboo straws rather than plastic. When you must use disposable plastic items, recycle them whenever possible.

Seeing Hawksbills in Papua New Guinea

In Papua New Guinea, the family-owned Walindi Plantation Resort on the shore of Kimbe Bay caters to divers enjoying the Kimbe Bay reefs. Accommodations include 12 traditional-style, self-contained bungalows along the shoreline and eight Plantation House Rooms surrounded by rainforest gardens. A central area includes a restaurant, bar, swimming pool, sundeck, boutique, and library.

Three custom-built day dive boats take divers to moorings on more than 40 dive sites. A recent coral survey in this bay counted 413 species of hard coral—more than half the total species in the entire world.

Walindi also offers live-aboard diving on the M/V *FeBrina*, which cruises from the resort to dive sites such as Witu Islands, Fathers Reefs, South Coast New Britain, and Rabaul. Resort owner Cecile Benjamin, a member of the Women Divers Hall of Fame, says guests see hawksbills on a regular basis on both land-based and live-aboard dive trips.

Travel Information

Walindi Plantation Resort: +675 7234–8460, http://walindifebrina.com/

Travel tip Check the CDC website for recommended precautions to protect yourself from mosquito-borne illnesses.

Places to See Nesting Hawksbills

Seeing a hawksbill sea turtle swimming in the ocean provides a real thrill, but so does watching females come ashore to nest or hatchlings emerging from the sand. Places around the world offer the chance for this experience and the opportunity to also support organizations that work to protect the animals and their habitat. Sustainable projects operate in the following locations.

Maunabo, Puerto Rico: The local organization Amigos de las Tortugas Marinas offers turtle walks from the Mauna Caribe Hotel on weekends from April to June. Group size is limited, so reservations are recommended (Mauna Caribe Hotel: (787) 861–3330, http://tropicalinnspr.com/parador-maunacaribe).

Buck Island Reef National Monument, US Virgin Islands: Day trips to this park, open year-round from sunrise to sunset, are available from National Park Service concessionaires on St. Croix: (340) 773–1460, https://www.nps.gov/buis (look under "Plan Your Visit," then "Basic Information," then "Permits & Reservations" for a list of concessionaires).

Jack and Isaac Bays Preserve, St. Croix: In August and September, this Nature Conservancy Preserve offers guided tours at night to watch turtles nesting and scientists collecting data and, later in the season, to observe nest excavations. The beach is open year-round ((340) 718–5575, https://www.nature.org/ourinitiatives/regions/caribbean/virginislands/placesweprotect/us-virgin-islands-jack-and-isaac-bays.xml).

Bahia Jiquilisco Biosphere Preserve, El Salvador: The Eastern Pacific Hawksbill Initiative (ICAPO) works in this UNESCO preserve on the country's southeastern Pacific coast to protect nesting hawksbills. The organization welcomes visitors and accepts volunteers for one to four weeks (http://hawksbill.org/projects/map/bahia-jiquilisco-biosphere-reserve-el-salvador/).

Padre Ramos Nature Reserve, Nicaragua: On organized trips July to October, spend a week working with researchers from Fauna and Flora International, patrolling beaches for nests and participating in research in the small town of Padre Ramos. Trip includes lodging at the Fauna and Flora Nicaragua research station, a house on the estuary, meals, and activities (http://seethewild.org/nicaragua-sea-turtle-research/).

Ningaloo Reef, Western Australia: Hawksbills nest from November to March in the 180-mile-long Ningaloo Marine Park, part of a World Heritage Site. During nesting season, the Department of Environment and Conservation offers Turtle Interaction Evenings at the Jurabi Turtle Centre near Exmouth Township (http://ningalooturtles.org.au/jurabi.html).

Arnavons Community Marine Conservation Area, Solomon Islands: This 40,000-acre marine preserve, established with the help of the Nature Conservancy, sees hawksbill nesting year-round. That equals good chances of seeing one on a visit (www.arnavons.com/).

Yellow-eyed penguin in New Zealand
Credit: Samantha Elizabeth Tasker

Yellow-eyed Penguin

Megadyptes antipodes

Dunedin, New Zealand

PENGUIN PLACE

This tall, elegant penguin sports a band of pale yellow feathers around its head and eyes and yellow flecks on the top of its head, chin, and cheeks along with a slate-blue back and tail and white chest and belly. Juveniles lack the yellow headband and have paler eyes. Males are larger, but otherwise, the two sexes look the same.

Yellow-eyed penguins breed on the southeastern coast of New Zealand's South Island and on Stewart Island and its offshore islands, Auckland Islands, and Campbell Islands. It is the last living member of its genus. In New Zealand, yellow-eyed penguins also go by the name hoiho.

Solitary breeders, these birds make shallow, bowl-like nests from twigs, grass, and leaves, putting them just about anywhere, in forest and scrub along the coast, in open pasture, among trees planted by people as windbreaks, and even on exposed cliffs. Typically, surrounding vegetation conceals them from neighboring nests. Females lay three to five eggs mid-September to mid-October, and once the second egg is laid, the parents take turns incubating the eggs for between 39 and 51 days. Eggs hatch in early November, and chicks begin to fledge in mid-February to mid-March. At first, chicks are constantly brooded, but later the parents leave them alone during the day.

These birds forage as far as 15 miles offshore, diving to depths of more than 390 feet to catch a variety of fish, including red cod, sprat, sil-

Yellow-eyed penguins in southern New Zealand
Credit: Samantha Elizabeth Tasker

versides, blue cod, and squid. This species is thought to live an average of 8 years, but some have lived as long as 25 years.

As do other penguin species, yellow-eyed penguins have feathers forming a waterproof layer that protects their bodies in the ocean and, on land, creates a layer of air as insulation around the body. Their wings are modified into paddlelike flippers, with flat, broad bones and an almost-fused elbow and wrist joint to form a tapered, flat swimming flipper. Penguins spend roughly 60 percent of their lives at sea and can see better underwater than above it. The birds can even drink seawater.

Penguins' legs are set far back on their body, which streamlines their bodies for swimming. This also causes them to walk upright with short steps or hops, sometimes assisted by their bills or tails on steep climbs. In February and March, the birds molt and must remain on land while new feathers grow in, which takes about three weeks. They fatten up beforehand and may lose almost nine pounds of body weight during molting.

Threats to Yellow-eyed Penguins

This species ranks as Endangered on the IUCN Red List because of its very small breeding range and decline in quality of the forest and scrub habitat in which it nests (www.iucnredlist.org/details/22697800/0). Yellow-eyed penguins are not listed in any CITES appendices.

Estimates place the population at around 1,700 breeding pairs, the majority on Auckland and Campbell Islands. More than 600 pairs occupy the South Island, and at least 180 pairs live on and around Stewart Island. Hoiho are considered by New Zealand to be Threatened and Nationally Vulnerable. In general, yellow-eyed penguins are recognized as one of the most endangered penguin species.

Introduced ferrets, cats, and pigs prey on the birds' eggs and chicks. Adults are safe from these terrestrial predators, but not from dogs, which prey on chicks, juveniles, and adults. Commercial and recreational fisheries do not appear to have a direct effect on the availability of the yellow-eyed penguin's food sources, but the birds are caught as bycatch and drown in fishing nets. Loss and fragmentation of habitat caused by human activity represent a major threat.

The chicks can suffer from two diseases: avian diphtheria or diphtheritic stomatitis, a bacterial infection of the mouth; and *Leucocytozoon*, a protozoan that parasitizes the blood and organs. Avian malaria or biotoxins also may have affected populations, along with food shortages due to sea temperature changes. Crowds of tourists visiting breeding colonies may cause adults to delay landing on the beach to feed their chicks, leading fledglings to become underweight and potentially affecting their survival. Researchers have found that chicks that frequently miss meals weigh significantly less at the time they fledge than those from sites without human disturbance. In lean years, a missed meal could be life or death for a chick. Accidental fires also kill these penguins.

Seeing Penguins in New Zealand

Penguin Place, founded in 1985, is a private conservation reserve protecting this species. Its funding comes entirely from guided tour fees. The property supports a working sheep farm, but the owners have planted hundreds of native trees and shrubs for the penguins and installed nest boxes. Introduced animals are removed from the property, and injured or sick birds are provided with care.

Penguin tours include a presentation on the birds and how the project is helping them. Small groups travel by bus to the preserve area, where a guide leads walks through a system of covered trenches into viewing blinds. These allow guests to observe the birds in their living and breeding areas and to take up-close photographs without disturbing the animals. The tour lasts about an hour and a half and guarantees penguin sightings.

Tours run from 10:15 to 5:45 daily during summer, October to March, with one tour daily at 3:45 during winter, April to September.

From September through April, Penguin Place Lodge offers farm-stay accommodations, with a shared kitchen, laundry, and TV room, and private single, twin, or double rooms.

The Otago Peninsula, on the eastern coast of New Zealand's South Island, bills itself as the country's wildlife capital. The peninsula and harbor host an abundance of wildlife in addition to hoiho, including the royal albatross and seal colonies of Taiaroa Head, just a short distance from Penguin Place, and blue penguins at Pukekura. Visitors can also see the extremely rare New Zealand sea lion and, occasionally, sea elephants and Stewart Island shags.

Travel Information

Penguin Place, Otago, New Zealand: 64-3-478-0286, http://
penguinplace.co.nz/

Africa

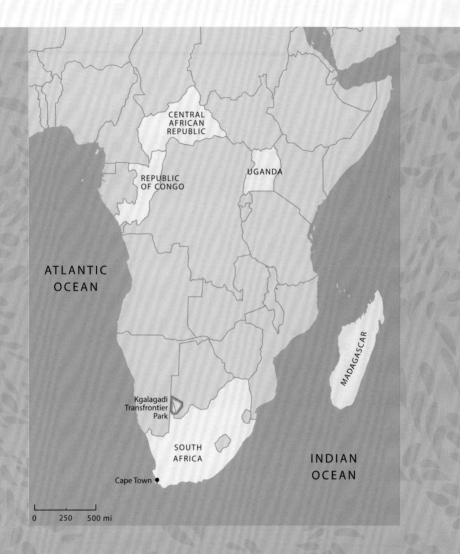

CENTRAL
AFRICAN
REPUBLIC

REPUBLIC
OF CONGO

UGANDA

ATLANTIC
OCEAN

MADAGASCAR

Kgalagadi
Transfrontier
Park

SOUTH
AFRICA

Cape Town

INDIAN
OCEAN

0   250   500 mi

A male African lion in the Kalahari

Credit: Jaco Powell

African Lion

Panthera leo

Kgalagadi Transfrontier Park, South Africa

KALAHARI SAFARIS

Lions appear often in human stories and tales, from Aslan in C. S. Lewis's *Chronicles of Narnia* to *The Lion King* and *The Wizard of Oz*. These powerful creatures personify bravery, leadership, and courage. No wonder many nature lovers have seeing lions on their bucket lists.

Lions live in many parts of Africa and some places in Asia. True to their reputation as large and fierce, lions reach heights of 4 feet, lengths up to 8 feet, and weigh as much as 500 pounds. They typically live 10 to 14 years. For short distances, these agile cats can run at a top speed of 50 miles per hour.

Lions prefer the savanna's open scrub and grass complexes and open woodland, but also inhabit forested areas, dry forests, bushlands, and deserts. Essentially, they just need enough shelter and cover to hunt and den. Lions are mainly nocturnal—active at night—and crepuscular—active at dawn and dusk. They rest for large parts of the day and night, typically active for only around four to six hours per day.

The most social of the cat species, lions live in complex groups called prides; members of a pride exhibit affection by touching, head rubbing, licking, and purring. A pride claims group territory, with both sexes defending territory against intruders of their same sex. An average lion pride numbers from 12 to 16 animals, with a core unit of four to six adult lionesses, two or more males that defend the pride, and a number of dependent cubs or subadults. Males compete fiercely for prides, and when new males take over a pride, they usually kill any cubs younger than 12 months of age. Lion trivia: Male lions frequently announce their presence with roars that can be heard up to six miles away.

The size of a pride and its territory depend greatly on availability of prey and water. Lions can get most of the water they need from prey and even plants, however, which makes it possible for them to tolerate very dry environments and to go a long time without drinking. Still, water sources play an important role in where they go and how they hunt, and lions typically spend most of their time close to water and even make most kills close to a water hole or riverbank.

Lions breed and have cubs any time of the year, so when prey is abundant, prides can quickly increase in size. They also may shrink their home range, which makes it possible for new prides to form. Only a few male lions are able to hold a territory and breed at younger than five years of age. Females typically begin reproducing at three years of age, having cubs every two to three years, depending on cub survival. Gestation lasts 100 to 114 days. Females in one pride often give birth around the same time and rear their young together, with cub survival best in prides with three to seven lionesses.

Male subadults usually leave the pride around age three or four years, but a pride takeover can force them out earlier. Most females remain with the pride into which they were born, but about a third disperse as well, usually between two and three years of age.

Females do most of the hunting, mainly at night and working as a team. They prefer medium to large ungulates such as wildebeest, zebra, buffalo, and kudu, but they catch smaller antelopes such as gazelles and impala as well and larger prey such as lost young or weakened adult rhinos and elephants. Lions sometimes kill unattended livestock, steal the kills of other predators, and scavenge carcasses.

Based on recent genetic studies, the IUCN Species Survival Commission Cat Specialist Group proposed two subspecies of lions: *P.1. leo* in Asia and West, Central, and North Africa; and *P.1. melanochaita* in South and East Africa.

A female African lion with her cub
Credit: Jaco Powell

Threats to Lions

The African lion is classified as Vulnerable on the IUCN Red List (www.iucnredlist.org/details/15951/0). South African lions are listed as Least Concern, but those in West Africa are listed as Critically Endangered. It is listed in CITES Appendix II. In 2015, the US FWS listed the subspecies *P.1. leo* as Endangered under the ESA and *P. 1. melanochaita* as Threatened.

Lions once roamed across Africa, Europe, the Middle East, and southwestern Asia. They disappeared in the first century from Europe and disappeared in North Africa, the Middle East, and most parts of Asia between 1800 and 1950. Only a small Asian population remains.

Recent estimates place the African lion population at about 35,000 lions—a decline of more than 50 percent since 1980—occupying less than 20 percent of their former range. West Africa's isolated lion subpopulation totals an estimated 400 individuals. It is regionally extinct in Côte d'Ivoire, Gambia, Guinea-Bissau, Mali, Mauritania, Sierra Leone, and Togo and may be extinct in Ghana and Guinea.

Main threats include habitat loss, loss of prey, poaching, retaliatory killings by humans (worsened by an increasing human population), and weak regulation and management of protected areas. An indirect threat comes from the combination of distemper outbreaks and severe drought caused by climate change. While lions usually shake off this disease, during the drought, their prey became weakened by malnutrition and infested with ticks. The lions then ate the ticks, which carried a blood parasite that rendered them less able to cope with distemper. Droughts likely will become more commonplace as the climate warms.

Trophy hunting also plays a role in the lion's decline. The FWS estimated there were 11 million big game hunters in the United States in 1996. A 2005 report put the number of registered big game hunters in Europe at 6.8 million, with 1.3 million believed to hunt abroad.

According to TRAFFIC, an organization that tracks the international trade of wildlife, almost 16,000 trophy hunts took place in 2000 in Namibia alone. These hunts involved a wide variety of species—birds, reptiles, mammals, and even primates—both endangered and not, including four of the so-called African big five: Cape buffalo, leopard, rhinoceros, and lion. TRAFFIC also documented 5,575 trophy hunts in 2001 in South Africa, Namibia, Botswana, Zimbabwe, and Tanzania. Between 1999 and 2008, at least 5,663 trophies of wild lions alone were legally traded internationally, 64 percent of them imported to the United States.

Some claim this industry has a positive economic effect for countries where the hunting occurs, estimating the overall economic impact of trophy hunting worldwide anywhere from $10 million to $200 million per year. But a study commissioned by Born Free USA, Humane Society International, the Humane Society of the United States, and the International Fund for Animal Welfare (IFAW) in 2013 suggested trophy hunting actually makes a minimal contribution to incomes in the countries where it occurs.

Furthermore, Jeff Flocken, North American regional director for the IFAW, points out that hunting brings in much less revenue than wildlife viewing. "From an economics point of view, while an individual hunt may bring in a large amount of revenue that one time, much more can be made in sustainable, ethical, long-term wildlife viewing," he says. "Revenue to Africa from hunts measures in the millions; wildlife viewing measures in the billions."

Flocken points to the case of Cecil, a well-known and popular lion in Zimbabwe's Hwange National Park, killed by a US trophy hunter in 2015. "Thousands of people came to the park just to see him. After this kill, he won't generate any more income for the area." In July 2017, a trophy hunter killed Xanda, one of about a dozen surviving offspring fathered by Cecil. The six-year-old male lion wore a tracking collar and had wandered about a mile outside Hwange National Park.

In addition, legal hunting can serve to provide a cover for illegal activities. Xanda's killer was completely within the law, but in Cecil's case, while it appears the hunter had legal permits, Flocken says he may have used them illegally. Further, the trophy-hunting industry lends legitimacy to having a lion head or elephant tusk on the wall and possibly fuels demand for poached products. Trophy hunting may not be the biggest threat, but clearly it is a threat.

Trophy hunting has been a mechanism for protecting land in areas unsuitable for wildlife viewing and other forms of ecotourism, and trophy hunting bans in Kenya, Tanzania, and Zambia actually seem to be associated with increased loss of wildlife. But the IUCN notes that trophy hunting has not proven to be an important conservation tool in key African lion-hunting countries, because benefits from lion hunts are not directed to local communities.

The FWS found that some trophy-hunting programs lack a basis in science or are not sustainably managed, so the agency created a permitting mechanism to support and strengthen the accountability of conservation programs in other nations. This mechanism allows people to import *P. 1. melanochaita*, including sport-hunted trophies, "from countries with established conservation programs and well-managed lion populations."

Loss of habitat is a more significant problem for African wildlife—only 22 percent of the lion's historic range remains, for example—and poaching may be the gravest threat of all. "By its very nature, wildlife poaching is hard to quantify because the activity is illegal, underground, and not always uncovered," says Adam M. Roberts, CEO of the Born Free Foundation. "What we do know for certain is that the effect of poaching on wildlife populations is profound." Poaching and the illegal wildlife trade, which includes elephant ivory, rhino horn, and lion skins and bones, may net as much as $10 billion a year, according to the World Wildlife Fund. Increasingly, lions are poached for use in traditional Asian medicine, which formerly used tiger bones and body parts. With tiger populations declining, that trade sees lions as an alternative.

How You Can Help

Support lion research and conservation at the University of Oxford, which had followed the movements of Cecil in minute detail since 2008. Sign up for updates and donate at www.wildcru.org/support-us/.

Seeing Lions in the Kgalagadi

Options for seeing lions and supporting their conservation include safari-style guided trips and volunteer expeditions.

Kalahari Safari Tours

The 9.1-million-acre Kgalagadi Transfrontier Park occupies the corner of South Africa between Namibia and Botswana in the southern Kalahari Desert. The Kgalagadi were some of the first people to penetrate the northern Kalahari, and its name comes from the Kgalagadi word *Makgadikgadi*, meaning "saltpans" or "great thirstland."

The park, first formed in 1931, expanded in 1935 and 1938, took in Mabuasehube Game Reserve in 1971, and was incorporated into Gemsbok National Park in 1992. Its residents include the black-maned Kalahari lions, springboks, gemsboks, wildebeests, hyenas, leopards, cheetahs, mongooses, meerkats, eagles, and more. Those on night drives regularly see African wild cats and bat-eared foxes. The bushman grass and camelthorn tree landscape makes for excellent wildlife watching here. Highlights are watching predators such as lions, cheetahs, leopards, and hyenas, as well as seasonal movements of large herbivores, including blue wildebeests, springboks, elands, and red hartebeests. Other special sightings include honey badgers and pangolins, or scaly anteaters.

Kalahari Safari—Cape Fox Tours, based in South Africa, offers tours in the Kgalagadi. Trips begin at the Upington airport, and a typical itinerary includes a stop at Augrabies Falls National Park to view one of the six largest waterfalls in the world, followed by a game drive through the park, stops at scenic overlooks on the Orange River Gorge, and an overnight in on-site chalets. On day two, the tour travels to Kgalagadi Transfrontier Park for a late-afternoon game drive. The next three days include early-morning and late-afternoon game drives, picnic lunches, nature walks with local guides, night game drives, 4 x 4 trails in the sand dunes, and dinner under the stars around the campfire.

Guide Jaco Powell, a zoologist, entomologist, and South Africa National Parks honorary ranger, reports that the most common and abundant animals seen include springbok, gemsbok or oryx, blue wildebeest, and ostrich. Best sightings occur very early in the morning and late in the afternoon.

Lion sightings vary, but a good morning might include encounters with three different prides of lions. Some of them may have as many as 23 members. "We often find them walking toward the water holes," Powell says. "The younger animals will play and practice their hunting skills on one another. We sometimes follow lions as they hunt, and the open terrain usually gives us a good, unobstructed view of what they are doing."

Later in the day, the lions sleep under trees and rest until it starts to cool down. People on his tours often hear lions roaring close by. Tours often find cheetahs hunting and leopards close to the road, along with honey badgers, cape foxes, caracals, and meerkats.

Volunteering with Lions in Kenya

Earthwatch offers 14-day volunteer expeditions in Kenya. Volunteers help researchers record the locations and abundance of zebras, cattle, and other herbivores in the Ol Pejeta Conservancy, where six prides of lions live. These lions wear radio collars used to track their movements. Comparing this tracking data with observation of herbivores shows the specific prey species these cats follow. Volunteers also help check camera traps for hyenas and leopards, sorting through the images to identify individual animals.

Ol Pejeta Conservancy, created in 1989 to provide sanctuary for black rhinos from elsewhere in Kenya, now contains one of the country's largest black rhino populations. It also houses much other wildlife in addition to lions, hyenas, zebras, and rhinos, including giraffes, gazelles, waterbucks, cheetahs, vervet monkeys, and many bird species. Most residents of the Laikipia Plateau around it ranch cattle and sheep.

Some afternoons, volunteers spend time entering data in Ol Pejeta's research center, and they often have the opportunity to work with locals, as the researchers prioritize hiring people in the area, especially women, as field scouts, and work with nearby schools to expose students to conservation and science careers. Many evenings include free time.

This research project seeks to include livestock production as part of any conservation solution. This comes from growing recognition that national parks typically provide too little space for viable populations of large predators and that setting aside vast wilderness areas that exclude humans and livestock is impractical. Rather, wildlife conservation needs to be made compatible with human economies.

Travel Information

Kalahari Safari: jacelstours@mweb.co.za, http://kalaharisafari.com/
Kgalagadi Transfrontier Park: https://www.sanparks.org/parks/kgalagadi/
Earthwatch Exploring Lions and Their Prey in Kenya: http://earthwatch.org/expeditions/exploring-lions-and-their-prey-in-kenya

Travel tips The best time to visit South Africa is the summer months of January through March when nights are short, limiting the dark hours for hunting, and high temperatures increase the frequency of visits to water holes. Expect hot temperatures. Earthwatch sends teams into the field in Kenya January through September; the hottest temperatures occur in February and the coolest in June. Check the CDC website for the latest status on mosquito-borne illnesses. Check the US State Department website for travel alerts and travel warnings.

African penguins on Boulders Beach, Cape Town, Western Cape Province, South Africa

Credit: South African Tourism

African Penguin

Spheniscus demersus

Cape Town, South Africa

JORVAN TOURS

The African continent's only breeding penguin species, these medium-sized birds have black backs and heads and a white belly with black spots and lines in a pattern unique to each individual. Juveniles have a slate-blue back that gradually darkens in two or three years into the black-and-white facial pattern of adults.

This species also goes by the name jackass penguin, as their loud, braying call sounds like a donkey's, and their large, noisy breeding colonies make quite an impression. Mated pairs return to the same nesting site year after year, and while they have no fixed breeding season, more nesting occurs between March and May than in other months in South Africa. Females lay two eggs in bowl-shaped depressions they dig in the sand, called burrows. Parents form tight bonds and take turns incubating their eggs for about 40 days, using a brood patch, or bare skin on the lower abdomen, that transfers heat to the eggs. They feed their chicks for two to four months. This species lives 10 to 15 years.

African penguins eat fish such as anchovies and sardines, swimming at speeds of as much as 12 miles per hour in the water and diving for more than two minutes to depths of almost 200 feet to catch their prey. Their waterproof coats need constant preening to distribute a waxy substance from the base of the tail. The birds come ashore to molt for 20 days between November and January, completely replacing their plumage.

Small muscles at the base of each feather allow penguins to keep their feathers tightly against their body, forming a waterproof layer, while in the water. On land, the muscle is used to keep feathers erect to trap an insulating layer of air. Their wings have flat, broad elbow bones and a nearly fused wrist joint, forming a tapered, flat flipper for swimming. Short, scalelike feathers cover each flipper. Penguins spend roughly 60 percent of their lives at sea and can see better underwater than above it. The birds can even drink seawater.

Short, strong legs set far back on the body make them more stream-lined while swimming and also cause them to stand and walk upright. Penguins move in short steps or hops, using their bills or tails for assistance when climbing steep slopes. In the water, African penguins are hunted by sharks and fur seals, and, on land, nesting penguins and young may be eaten by seagulls, mongoose, and cats.

African penguins on Boulders Beach, Cape Town, Western Cape Province, South Africa   Credit: South African Tourism

Threats to African Penguins

The US FWS listed African penguins as Endangered under the ESA in 2010. The African penguin is listed in CITES Appendix II and on IUCN's Red List as Endangered (www.iucnredlist.org/details/22697810/0). In fact, the IUCN considers 5 of the world's 18 penguin species Endangered, 5 more penguin species as Vulnerable, and another 5 as Near Threatened. Only 3 species still have healthy enough numbers to qualify for its Least Concern classification.

The current size of the African penguin population is only 10 percent of its numbers more than 100 years ago. The decrease originally resulted from overcollection of penguin eggs for human food and collection of their guano for fertilizer. Today, commercial fishing represents a major threat, particularly overfishing and concentrated fishing efforts near penguin colonies for forage species such as Antarctic krill. When commercial fishing grounds overlap with penguin foraging grounds, this can make it more difficult for penguins to find nourishment, according to the Pew Charitable Trusts, a nonprofit that focuses on ocean conservation.

Habitat destruction also takes a toll on these birds. Destruction occurs due to tourism-related activities, such as foot traffic and litter, and oil spills, which affect not only foraging habitat but the health of individual colonies of penguins. Climate change and resulting sea ice melting may represent the greatest threat to struggling penguin populations (earthtalk.org/penguins-on-the-brink/). All breeding areas in South Africa are protected as national parks or nature reserves, and collection of guano or eggs is no longer permitted.

How You Can Help

In addition to supporting conservation tourism operations, you can help protect and conserve African penguins several other ways.

Adopt a Penguin

Symbolically adopt an African penguin or donate to help rescue birds from oil spills through the Southern African Foundation for the Conservation of Coastal Birds (sanccob.co.za/). Winter storms and winds carry oil leaks from ships or faulty pipelines straight into the penguin colonies, the organization reports. This oil breaks through the birds' waterproof feathers and prevents them from swimming, which means they cannot feed. Without help, they would starve to death. SANCCOB rescues the birds, washing them with soap and brushes and providing them with heat lamps, fish and vitamins, and veterinary care. SANCCOB also provides incubators for chicks and eggs abandoned by oiled adults. The organization needs volunteers to help clean, feed, and care for birds and to help with education and marketing efforts.

Be a Citizen-Scientist

Anyone with a computer can help scientists who study penguins and their habitats. Citizen-scientists scan images from more than 100 sites and mark individual adult penguins, chicks, and eggs in each photo. Participants also mark other animals present in the photos so scientists can see how often these animals are near nests (https://www.penguin watch.org/?_ga=1.167220542.1230673867.1470002842).

Seeing Penguins in South Africa

Boulders Penguin Colony, established in 1983 and part of Table Mountain National Park on the Cape of Good Hope, shelters about 2,000 African penguins. This section of the enormous park includes three beaches, a penguin viewing area, and three boardwalks that allow people to watch the birds with minimal disturbance of the colony. The boardwalks overlook beaches and rocky areas where penguins hang out, and visitors can linger as long as they like watching and photographing the birds. The park has restrooms and outdoor showers as well.

The penguins also come onto the beach, where immense boulders provide shelter from currents, wind, and large waves both on the sand and in the shallow water. If you encounter penguins on the beach or rocks, do not touch or feed them—their beaks are sharp, and they may nip if they feel threatened.

Full-day trips with Jorvan Tours departing from Cape Town include a stop at the Boulders Penguin Colony in addition to Clifton and Camps Bay Beaches, the Twelve Apostles, Chapmans Peak scenic drive, Cape of Good Hope Nature Reserve, Cape Point, and Simon's Town. One of the country's oldest settlements, Simon's Town now is home to South Africa's main naval base. Its picturesque Victorian buildings, quaint streets, and walkways include a number of museums, including a naval museum, along with shops, restaurants, a harbor, and swimming beaches. Half-day tours include the penguin colony, Cape of Good Hope Nature Reserve, Cape Point, Simon's Town, and Muizenberg surfer's paradise.

"The story goes that a pair of penguins arrived at Boulders Beach in 1983, laid their first eggs in 1985, and decided to stay," says Jorvan owner Brian Vandayar. He explains that the birds used to have access to the town and the residences and would lie underneath cars to keep warm and enter shops and gardens, becoming a bit of a stinky nuisance and putting themselves in danger. Even worse, though, people moved eggs, stepped on nests, and tried to touch or hold the birds for photos. The population began to decline, so in 2003 the national park service fenced off the beach to prevent the penguins from leaving it for their own protection.

People on the tours see the birds every day of the year. "The boardwalk allows everyone to enjoy the penguins but not interfere with their daily lives," Vandayar says. "We spend anywhere from thirty minutes to several hours watching these cuties play around on the beach and in the sea, but on average, most people stay thirty to forty-five minutes."

These tours accommodate between two and seven people, and Jorvan also offers private tours, with a more flexible schedule allowing additional time at the colony or other stops. Jorvan Tour's slogan is "Passionate about Cape Town," and Brian and his wife, Melanie Vandayar, have both lived there since childhood. They emphasize ethics and professionalism and love sharing their hometown with visitors. They established a social responsibility program in 2006 that supports a total of 10 township projects in Cape Town. This includes offering a residence to up to 12 disadvantaged students, providing room, board, a place to study, and encouragement and support. Jorvan also offers tours of the townships, including visits to the school and meeting students in person. Those who wish may make a donation to help support the program or sponsor an individual student for a school year.

Travel Information

Jorvan Tours, Cape Town: +27-21-371-4469, jorvantours@telkomsa .net, http://jorvantours.co.za/

Travel tips Summer (December through February) is peak season and is crowded and hot. Autumn (March, April, and May) and spring (September to November) are cooler and much less crowded.

Black-and-white ruffed lemur, Mantadia, Madagascar

Credit: Frank Vassen

Black-and-white Ruffed Lemur

Varecia variegata

Madagascar, Africa

MOUNTAIN TRAVEL SOBEK AND TERRA INCOGNITA ECOTOURS

More than 70 different species of lemurs live on the island of Madagascar, the world's fourth largest. It drifted 250 miles away from mainland Africa into the Indian Ocean some 88 million years ago, creating isolation and unique evolutionary forces resulting in plant and animal species that are 90 percent endemic, or found only on this island, including lemurs.

The black-and-white ruffed lemur, also called simply the ruffed lemur, lives in lowland to mid-altitude rain forests in eastern Madagascar. Scientists identify three subspecies. Ruffed lemurs have a mostly black face with a furry ruff from the ears to the neck, white in the case of this species and red in its closest relative, red ruffed lemurs (*V. rubra*). Both have long, caninelike muzzles and a significant overbite.

Few people have studied ruffed lemurs in the wild, but observers report groups as small as a mated pair and their offspring and as large as 16 individuals, including adults of both sexes. Group members use a common home range and defend it from neighboring groups. Lemurs have several different calls, and group members call in chorus. Ruffed lemurs have loud roar or shriek choruses used to coordinate group movement and warn other group members of predators.

Females form the core of lemur groups and are the main defenders of territory. In fact, female ruffed lemurs and ring-tailed lemurs have social dominance in feeding and other contexts. Females typically prevail in aggressive interactions between males and females, although black-and-white ruffed lemur females do occasionally show submission and typically must be more aggressive to win these confrontations.

Ruffed lemurs sleep, forage, travel, and feed in trees, seeming to prefer large trees and the upper half to upper third of the forest canopy. Not surprisingly, they eat mostly fruit, nectar, and pollen along with small amounts of leaves and seeds during the dry season when fruit and nectar are scarce. To eat nectar, lemurs stick their long noses deep into flowers, picking up and transporting pollen on their snouts and serving as important pollinators for certain species of plants.

Members of the primate family, lemurs recklessly hurl themselves from one tree to another, twisting in midair and landing lower down in neighboring trees, making spectacular crashing sounds. Ruffed lemurs dangle from small terminal branches of a tree to feed, grasping slender branches with their feet. They also do this to engage in play wrestling or mutual grooming with other lemurs. Ruffed lemurs suspend themselves in this way more commonly than other lemurs. Ruffed lemurs are considered arboreal quadrupeds, meaning they use all four legs to travel through trees. They also move on all fours on the ground, using bounding hops with their tails held high.

These lemurs breed between May and July. Females gestate for 102 days and give birth to litters of two or three in September and October. Lemurs are the only primates to keep their young in nests, which are hidden high up in trees. Infants are not able to grasp their mother, so she will pick them up and move them one at a time in her mouth. After a week or two, the mother usually removes them from the nest, parking them in a tree while she forages nearby. By three or four weeks of age, the young can follow their mother on their own. Despite their tree-top lifestyle, 65 percent of ruffed lemurs die from accidental falls and related injuries before three months of age.

This lemur's natural predators include the Henst's goshawk, fossa (pronounced foo-sa and made famous in the animated movie *Mada-*

gascar—"The fossa are attacking!"), and ring-tailed and brown-tailed mongoose.

Threats to Lemurs

The black-and-white ruffed lemur is considered Critically Endangered on the IUCN Red List and listed on CITES Appendix I. In all, 24 lemur species are now listed by IUCN as Critically Endangered, 49 Endangered, and 20 as Vulnerable (www.iucnredlist.org/details/22918/0).

A 2016 paper in *Science* magazine classified Madagascar's five endemic lemur families—species that occur nowhere else—as the most threatened mammal group on earth. Some 94 percent of the more than 100 lemur species are threatened, with some populations falling to fewer than 500 animals. All animals play important ecological roles; lemurs are critical in maintaining the island's forests. Loss of these species could trigger "extinction cascades," decreasing reproduction of trees and affecting other species that depend on trees.

A political crisis in the country in 2009 made things worse for lemurs, and the authors of the paper call for adoption of an emergency action plan put forth by the IUCN. The plan names 30 priority sites and highlights three major strategies, including community-based, protected-habitat management; promotion of ecotourism; and the presence of researchers in the country to train locals in conservation and deter illegal activities. Accomplishing these goals will require foreign financial aid. Of course, people do not have to wait for this to happen to visit the country and support existing ecotourism.

Much ruffed lemur habitat has been affected by slash-and-burn agricultural practices, logging, and mining, and habitat loss represents the principal threat to their survival. The animals also suffer from unsustainable hunting pressure. With large bodies and diurnal habits (meaning they move about during the day), they are targeted by human hunters more than other lemur species and often the first to disappear when people encroach on their habitat. Hunters often simply listen for the animals' vocalizations to find them. Many are captured to be kept or sold as pets.

How You Can Help

Duke University in North Carolina operates the Duke Lemur Center, the world's largest lemur sanctuary outside Madagascar. Tour options include regular one-and-one-half-hour tours, twilight tours, Behind the Scenes, and Walking with Lemurs and Keeper for a Day, both of which take place inside the animal enclosures (http://lemur.duke.edu/visit/tours/).

Symbolically adopt one of Duke's lemurs to help cover the cost of care for that animal as well as to support the center's work in the United States, Madagascar, and around the world. Adopters receive regular updates and photos of the animal they choose, including black-and-white ruffed as well as well as other species (http://lemur.duke.edu/engage/donate/).

Seeing Lemurs in Madagascar

Two different tour outfitters offer trips in Madagascar that include seeing lemurs.

Mountain Travel Sobek

A tour by Mountain Travel Sobek (MTS) explores Madagascar's national parks and private reserves by boat, four-wheel drive, and foot, with accommodations in small resorts and deluxe eco-lodges. The group visits the Perinet Reserve, Grand Tsingy UNESCO World Heritage Site, and the lush rain forests of Andasibe-Mantadia National Park, home to 11 different species of lemurs and the iconic indri. The group also stays at a private sanctuary camp on the Manadare River, where guests see a number of different species of lemurs from boats and on hikes.

Tanya Rinaldi, director of Africa, Middle East, and Pacific programs at MTS notes that the organization carefully selected the private reserves on its itinerary. "Unfortunately, many people here like to have lemurs as pets or use them as tourist attractions in the cities, charging people to hold and photograph them," Rinaldi says. "Now, we have private places trying to rehabilitate them, but there are not a lot of wild areas where the animals can be released," since much of the country's rain forest has been lost.

In the national parks, the group goes out with local guides to track lemurs. "We usually start early in the morning and hike from four to six hours looking for them," Rinaldi says. "They move quite quickly, so you are constantly moving and looking for them. You can stand in one place and listen to them calling to each other. Sometimes, we will be surrounded by them and can sit back and just listen. We may only see them for about fifteen minutes, or we may sit and watch for a good couple of hours. These are wild lemurs doing their thing."

The private reserves work with locals, educating them about how tourism can help both people and wildlife. "The Malagasy are beautiful people with a fantastic culture, and they are happy to see you. But wildlife suffers and things are tough for the local people," Rinaldi adds. "By visiting, maybe you are helping to do something about it."

Terra Incognita Ecotours

Terra Incognita Ecotours offers lemur-focused trips to Madagascar that include visits to several different sites, including protected rain forest in Andasibe-Mantadia National Park and the Perinet Reserve. "At Andasibe-Mantadia National Park, we always see five or six different species of lemurs, including the indiri," says Terra Incognita's Ged Caddick. "They have a very distinctive song, a really haunting, melancholy call that travels for miles. We also see other wildlife such as chameleons, frogs, birds."

The tour then travels to the spiny desert of Berenty, home to bizarre desert trees that look like cacti. Here, Caddick says, the group sees ring-tailed and mouse lemurs and some nocturnal species. "The real hook here is the big lemurs that hop on two legs across the ground. We always see those and the ringtails. All lemurs are very approachable. They evolved in absence of predators and so are very tolerant of people getting close. They kind of carry on about their business without minding us."

The trip ends at Anjajavy private reserve on the west coast, which has a different array of lemur species. "We see lemurs there every day. The resort covers thousands of acres with many lemurs, many birds, and a beautiful coastline. For me, it is the highlight of the trip." Other endemic wildlife here include Coquerel's sifaka, lovebirds, Cuvier's spiny iguana, abundant malachite kingfishers, pygmy kingfishers, brown lemurs, and Madagascar fish eagles.

"It is a life-changing experience," Caddick says. "Madagascar has a different culture, spectacular scenery, friendly people, amazing wildlife. It is unlike anything found anywhere else on earth." In keeping with principles of responsible ecotourism, the outfitter employs local people, uses locally owned and operated lodges and outfitters, and buys local goods and services. It also makes a donation to the Lemur Conservation Foundation on each trip.

Travel Information

Mountain Travel Sobek: (888) 831-7526, http://mtsobek.com/regions/africa

Terra Incognita Ecotours: (855) 326-8687, http://ecotours.com/ecotour/madagascar-expedition-land-time-forgot

Travel tips The best time of year to visit is June and July. Coastal regions remain hot throughout the year. The central plateau has a temperate climate, with warm summers and cool winters. Average temperatures in Antananarivo on the plateau are 48 to 68 degrees Fahrenheit in July.

Eastern mountain gorilla
Credit: Richard Ruggiero, USFWS

Eastern Mountain Gorilla

Gorilla beringei

Uganda, Africa

NATURAL HABITAT ADVENTURES

A real, live King Kong, a mountain gorilla stands up to 5.5 feet tall, can weigh 440 pounds, and has large, muscular arms. These apes walk on their feet and the knuckles of their hands, with those arms providing balance and support for their large body. Gorillas have humanlike hands, with four broad fingers and an opposable thumb, and feet with five toes and an opposable big toe. Their Michael Phelps–like arm spans can total 6.5 feet. Each individual sports a distinctively shaped nose beneath a bulging forehead and high domed head. Mountain gorilla trivia: Mountain gorillas share almost 98 percent of their DNA with humans.

This species lives in forests at elevations of 8,000 to 13,000 feet, where temperatures often drop below freezing. They have long hair to help keep them warm. Mature males are called silverbacks for the silver color of the hair on their back and hips. A mountain gorilla social group usually includes one dominant silverback male, three adult females, and four or five offspring. Group territories physically overlap, with silverbacks defending their group rather than a specific territory.

These gorillas live 40 to 50 years. Females begin to have young around 10 years of age and have offspring four or more years apart. Gestation is about eight and a half months, and newborns weigh only about four pounds. Baby gorillas develop nearly twice as fast as human infants but nurse for more than three years.

Mountain gorillas include two populations that some scientists think should be considered as separate subspecies. About half of the population lives in Virunga National Park, Africa's first national park. Established in 1925, it covers much of the Virunga Mountains, a range made up of extinct volcanoes stretching through the Democratic Republic of Congo and Rwanda as well as Uganda. The other half of the population occupies Bwindi Impenetrable National Park in Uganda.

Primarily vegetarians, gorillas eat the leaves, shoots, and stems of a variety of plants. Unlike other primates, gorillas do not climb trees.

Gorilla Family Tree

Monkeys and apes are members of the order Primates; great apes and humans belong to the family Hominidae. The genus *Gorilla* includes two species: *beringei*, the eastern gorilla; and *gorilla*, the western gorilla. The species *beringei* includes two subspecies: *graueri* and *beringei*, the eastern mountain gorilla (*G. b. beringei*). The western gorilla species also includes two subspecies: *diehli* and *gorilla*, the western lowland gorilla (*G. g. gorilla*). Read about the western lowland gorilla in the next section.

Great apes differ from monkeys in several ways. They are larger, walk upright more often, and lack tails. Apes also have larger, more developed brains than monkeys do.

Threats to Eastern Mountain Gorillas

The IUCN Red List rated the mountain gorilla as Critically Endangered in 1996 and affirmed that status in 2000 and 2008 (www.iucnredlist .org/details/39999/0). It is listed in CITES Appendix I. The entire population totals only a few hundred individuals.

The eastern mountain gorilla is one subspecies of the eastern gorilla, *G. beringei*, the world's largest primate. (The taxonomic organization of the genus *Gorilla* is explained in the "Western Lowland Gorilla" section.) Fewer than 5,000 eastern gorillas remain, and the IUCN recently

Young eastern mountain gorilla
Credit: Dirck Byler, USFWS

changed the status of this species and both of its subspecies from Endangered to Critically Endangered.

According to the World Wildlife Fund, main threats to the mountain
gorilla's survival include habitat loss, disease, and poaching. Habitat
loss occurs as people clear land for agriculture and livestock—including
illegal clearing of land within protected areas—and harvest wood to produce charcoal, an illegal but sizable industry. Habitat loss worsened in
the 1990s after war in Rwanda and civil unrest in the Democratic Republic of Congo. Refugees from these conflicts entered gorilla habitat
around the Virunga Mountains, leading to destruction of habitat as well
as poaching of the animals.

Rebels that have taken over part of Virunga National Park interfere with conservation work and harm humans as well as gorillas. Since 1996, 140 of the park's rangers have been killed; in June 2015 alone, 2 rangers and 15 soldiers were ambushed and killed by two insurgent groups.

Contact with humans exposes gorillas to human diseases, which often cause more severe illness in these animals than in humans. Mountain gorillas can die from a plain old cold, for example. On the other hand, gorillas that have regular contact with researchers and tourists have higher survival than groups without contact. This is likely a result of increased protection from human presence as well as veterinary care available to sick and injured gorillas.

Poaching still represents a major threat to gorillas. People hunt mountain gorillas for meat and trophies and also capture live infants (often killing the mother in the process). During the civil war in Rwanda, people killed as many as 15 mountain gorillas. As large numbers of Rwandan refugees fled to camps along the outskirts of the park between 1990 and 1994, four silverback males and some of their group members were killed. These animals also can be caught and harmed when people set snares for other animals.

How You Can Help

More than 140 Virunga rangers have been killed in the past 10 years. When this happens, their spouses and children face the loss of what is usually their primary source of income. The Virunga Fallen Rangers Fund exists to help these families. The Thin Green Line Foundation protects endangered species and habitat by supporting park rangers and their families worldwide, providing rangers with antipoaching equipment and training and financial support to the surviving spouses and orphans of park rangers killed in the line of duty. Donate at https://virunga.org/donate/.

Seeing Mountain Gorillas in Uganda

Natural Habitat Adventures (NHA) and WWF offer a Great Uganda Gorilla Safari and a Gorilla Photo Safari as well as custom gorilla trips. Trips include treks through Uganda's Bwindi Impenetrable National Park for close-up encounters with mountain gorillas as well as observing wild chimpanzees in Kibale National Park and traditional African game in Queen Elizabeth National Park. "The great safari focuses on primates, and the ultimate gorilla photo safari is a photography-focused version with a guide who is a photographer as well as an expert on the animal. It also has a smaller group," says the outfitter's Wendy Redal.

The gorilla safari begins with two days in the Kibale Forest rainforest reserve, which has the highest concentration anywhere in the world of primates, including 500 chimpanzees. The group takes a morning "swamp walk," looking for more than 100 species of birds in a wetland sanctuary, followed by two walks with local trackers to look for chimps. Other wildlife that participants may see on these walks includes red colobus, black-and-white colobus, red tails, and gray-cheeked mangabey.

The tour spends three days in Queen Elizabeth National Park, located on the western side of the Rift Valley overlooking Lakes George and Edward and the Kazinga Channel, where hippos congregate in significant numbers. This park contains classic African game animals, including zebra, giraffe, lion, antelope, and buffalo.

Two days in Bwindi National Park follow. This, Redal says, ranks as one of the best places to see gorillas in the world. "There are three gorilla groups habituated to human contact. We split into two small groups with local trackers skilled at finding signs of their presence. It can take anywhere from an hour to half a day to locate them, but once we do, you spend a full hour sitting quietly observing a gorilla family. They observe us as well; it's an amazing, primal, magical encounter. Time just stands still while you're with them, mesmerized in their presence."

Gorilla treks involve intensive hiking through the rain forest, without trails, sometimes for three to four hours. Participants do not have to be extreme athletes but do need a reasonable level of physical fitness and ability to put up with the humidity. "Once you come face-to-face with the gorillas, all the hardship fades away," Redal promises. "The reward is so magnificent."

The photography safari includes four separate gorilla tracking expeditions, two in Uganda—Kibale National Park and Bwindi Impenetrable National Park and World Heritage Site—and two in Rwanda's Volcanoes National Park, where Dian Fossey conducted her groundbreaking research. The group also observes wild chimpanzees and other monkeys in Kibale National Park. A day and a half in Queen Elizabeth National Park provides viewing of traditional safari animals such as elephants, zebras, giraffes, and lions. This itinerary also features a full hour in close proximity to a gorilla family to observe and photograph these magnificent animals.

NHA expedition leaders are accomplished photographers, offering tips and advice throughout, and primate experts who have completed in-depth training with WWF scientists. The organization uses small, intimate camps and lodges in remote areas wherever possible, locations chosen for scenic settings, natural ambience, and proximity to wildlife —and lack of crowds.

On photography-based tours, the drives between safari locations offer opportunities to photograph the countryside and people along the way. Driving also avoids size and weight restrictions on small planes that can limit the amount of photography equipment.

Natural Habitat funds projects that reduce carbon emissions by an amount equivalent to that of the travel involved for its trips. Find more details about this program in the section on "Bengal Tigers."

Travel Information

Natural Habitat Adventures/World Wildlife Fund Great Uganda
  Gorilla Safari: (800) 543-8917, https://www.nathab.com/africa/
  the-great-african-primate-expedition/itinerary/

Natural Habitat Adventures/World Wildlife Fund Ultimate Gorilla
Photo Safari: (800) 543-8917, https://www.nathab.com/africa/
ultimate-gorilla-photo-safari/

Travel tips The best time of year to visit is June through November.
Weather is humid and occasionally rainy. Trekking with gorillas is a
strenuous activity on often uneven terrain. Participants must be physically able to participate.

Western lowland gorillas, orphaned as a result of the bushmeat and live infant trade, being rehabilitated for release in the wild by the Aspinall Foundation in Congo

Credit: Ian Redmond

Western Lowland Gorilla

Gorilla gorilla gorilla

Central African Republic and Republic of Congo

NATURAL WORLD SAFARIS

A subspecies of the western gorilla, western lowland gorillas live in lowland tropical forest, preferring areas of dense growth and swamp forests. The smallest of the gorillas, they stand 4 to 6 feet tall and weigh 150 to 400 pounds, as large as or larger than humans. Mature males, called silverbacks, have silver coloring that extends onto the legs and redder hair on their heads. Western lowland gorillas have a distinctive nose with a heart-shaped ridge around the nostrils.

Western lowland gorillas live in Cameroon, Central African Republic, Equatorial Guinea, Gabon, Congo, and Angola. The other subspecies is the Cross River gorilla (*G. g. diehli*).

This subspecies forms small groups, usually about 5 individuals, although a few groups as large as 10 or, rarely, 20 have been seen. Groups include an adult male, several adult females, and their offspring. The home range of a group may cover nearly eight square miles; group ranges overlap extensively, and the gorillas are not territorial. They may reproduce more slowly than mountain gorillas because of longer intervals between young and higher infant mortality.

Females have one infant, and a pregnancy is almost nine months. Newborns weigh about four pounds. They cling to their mothers' fur until about four months of age, then ride on their mothers' backs for up to three years. Between the ages of three and six, young gorillas spend their days playing, climbing and swinging in trees, and chasing each another. (This will sound familiar to many human parents.)

These apes eat roots, shoots, fruit, and tree bark and pulp. Western lowlands sleep on the ground in nests they build each night from branches and leaves, as do most gorillas. Recent research has shown that gorillas have the capacity to use tools; this species, for example, has been seen using a stick to test the depth of a river before deciding whether to cross. They are difficult to track and habituate to human presence due to their large home range and habit of moving constantly. They live 30 to 40 years.

Threats to Western Lowland Gorillas

The western gorilla, including both subspecies, is listed under the ESA as Endangered, included in CITES Appendix I, and listed as IUCN Critically Endangered (www.iucnredlist.org/details/9404/0). In fact, four of the six great apes are IUCN Critically Endangered—eastern gorilla, western gorilla, Bornean orangutan, and Sumatran orangutan. The IUCN lists chimpanzee and bonobo as Endangered.

Two main factors contributing to the decline of western gorillas include commercial hunting and the Ebola virus. Hunters had difficulty accessing the western lowland gorilla's range until the early 1980s due to lack of roads, but infrastructure improvements and depletion of timber elsewhere led to rapid increase in mechanized logging in areas where the gorillas live. Timber production in the region nearly doubled between 1991 and 2000, and the construction of logging roads into large areas of previously inaccessible forest gave hunters ready access to remote areas and the apes that live there, as well as access to markets. In addition, logging vehicles often transport bushmeat and logging workers frequently eat it.

The species' low reproductive rates cannot support even low levels of hunting, and the logging boom caused gorilla numbers to crash. Gabon alone saw an estimated 56 percent decline from 1983 to 2000, mostly attributed to hunting. Gabon has the lowest human population in the region, meaning hunting has an even higher impact elsewhere. Logging continues to threaten gorillas as rates of timber production continue to increase, primarily in areas that have not already been logged.

The Ebola virus causes repeated, massive gorilla and chimpanzee die-offs in remote areas, with outbreaks first noted in 1994 in northern Gabon. Minkébé National Park contained one of the world's largest protected populations of gorillas and chimpanzee before Ebola arrived. The virus struck populations in central Gabon in 1996, eastern Gabon in 2001, and areas of northwestern Congo in 2002 through 2005. Central Gabon was not monitored during these outbreaks but likely experienced ape die-offs as well.

Seeing Western Lowland Gorillas in Africa

Natural World Safaris offers trips to see lowland gorillas in the Central African Republic and Republic of Congo. The company emphasizes the extensive on-the-ground knowledge of its trip leaders, who have all lived, guided, or intimately explored the destinations where they work.

The Central African Republic trip includes tracking gorillas in the wild and observing other wildlife, including forest elephants and bongo. Travelers join the Ba'Aka pygmies on a net hunt, see hippos on canoe safaris, and take walking safaris to see primates, butterflies, and birds. The itinerary of necessity includes long transfers and long treks, but unique wildlife experiences reward the effort. The Central African Republic is a developing country with less infrastructure than, say, Kenya, but that, too, is part of the experience.

Tours visit Dzanga-Sangha National Park, home to some of Central African Republic's last untouched virgin rain forest and some of the most endangered animals in the world. The group often encounters forest elephants in the Dzanga *bai*, or clearing, and this area is home to black rhino and chimpanzees in addition to lowland gorillas.

Trekking after the gorillas involves crossing rivers and wading through long grasses and rain forests, in a way mimicking the life of these animals, which travel long distances each day to find food and a place to rest. "Lowland gorillas move around a lot more than mountain gorillas, so we move around a lot, too, and often tracking them takes longer," says Will Bolsover, managing director. "We have never not seen gorillas, but obviously they are wild animals, so we make no guarantees." Permits limit encounters to one hour once gorillas are found.

The Republic of Congo trip tracks western lowland gorillas in their natural habitat in Nouabale-Ndoki and Odzala-Kokoua National Parks and spends time with researchers in the area. On night walks in the forest, the group searches for unusual nocturnal primates such as galagos and pottos. Some itineraries combine gorilla tracking in Central African Republic and the Congo.

"You are putting money into projects on the ground in terms of local habitat, local infrastructure, local guides," Bolsover says. "Most of our guides are locals, so money goes directly into communities. Tours also bring stability into these areas; more eyes and more feet on the ground make questionable activities harder to undertake."

He calls seeing these animals in their natural habitat one of the best wildlife experiences there is. "Very rarely do you go into an animal's habitat on foot; usually you travel in a four by four. Here, you are with some of the largest primates on the planet, a two hundred-kilogram male gorilla, sort of the gentle giants of the wild world. It is definitely a breathtaking experience."

Travel Information

Natural World Safaris: https://www.naturalworldsafaris.com/wildlife/
    primates

Travel tips Check the CDC website for updates on measles outbreaks. Check the Department of State website for the latest travel alerts and warnings.

Europe

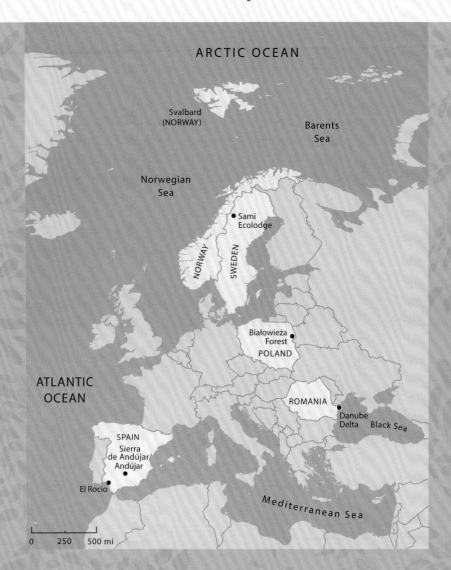

ARCTIC OCEAN

Svalbard
(NORWAY)

Barents
Sea

Norwegian
Sea

• Sami
Ecolodge

NORWAY

SWEDEN

Białowieża
Forest
POLAND

ATLANTIC
OCEAN

ROMANIA

Danube
Delta   Black Sea

SPAIN
Sierra
de Andújar/
Andújar

El Rocío

Mediterranean Sea

0   250   500 mi

Arctic fox in Churchill
Credit: Brad Josephs

Arctic Fox

Vulpes lagopus

Scandinavia

VARIOUS OUTFITTERS

Arctic foxes can hear prey beneath the snowpack. They leap into the air and pounce headfirst into the snow to catch a meal. Their wide, front-facing ears and incredible hearing make this neat trick possible.

The arctic fox lives in arctic and alpine tundra in Europe, Asia, North America and the Canadian archipelago, Siberian islands, Greenland, inland Iceland and the archipelago of Svalbard, and in subarctic maritime habitat in the Aleutian and Bering Seas, Commander Islands, and coastal Iceland.

Opportunistic predators and scavengers, arctic foxes rely on rodent populations, primarily lemmings. Those populations fluctuate, so the foxes also eat birds, reindeer, ptarmigan, and grouse, and those that live along ice-free coasts also prey on seabirds, seal carcasses, fish, and invertebrates. They will scavenge carrion left by larger predators such as polar bears, wolves, and wolverines.

Adaptations to their cold environment include compact bodies that minimize surface area; a short muzzle, ears, and legs to reduce heat loss; and deep, thick fur that keeps them warm. Thick fur on their paws allows them to walk on snow and ice. These foxes can swim, too. Individual animals have been known to travel nearly 500 miles from shore out over the pack ice and up to nearly 3,000 miles during one winter season.

Their coats, bright white in winter, become brown on their upperparts in summer with light gray or white underparts. Summer coats are half as

Arctic fox
Credit: Keith Morehead, USFWS

thick as in winter. A "blue" form occurs: a light brown coat with a bluish sheen in some areas in winter and in other areas, dark brown to black, becoming chocolate brown in summer.

Mating season usually lasts from early September to early May, and during this time, pairs are strongly territorial, marking the area and vocalizing frequently. Litter size varies between five and nine pups, depending on food supply. Arctic foxes usually mate for life and raise their young in complex dens. Some den sites are centuries old and have been used by numerous generations of foxes, growing quite large over time. The mother nurses her pups for the first three weeks while the male brings food. Once cubs begin to take meat, the female also hunts. Some pairs have helpers, usually their offspring from the previous year. Young leave the den at 8 to 10 weeks old and reach sexual maturity at 10 months.

Arctic foxes range from about 2 to 3.5 feet in length plus a 12-inch tail, standing 9 to 12 inches at the shoulder. Weight ranges from 6.5 to 21 pounds, with females typically smaller than males. Lifespan is three to six years. Red foxes, wolverines, and golden eagles prey on these foxes.

Threats to Arctic Foxes

Listed as Least Concern by IUCN Red List, the arctic fox is not considered Endangered under the ESA or included in a CITES appendix (www.iucnredlist.org/details/899/0). However, while the overall population likely contains several hundred thousand individuals, the population in mainland Scandinavia (Norway, Sweden, and Finland) may number fewer than 200. The arctic fox is considered Critically Endangered in Finland and seldom seen in the wild there.

In the past, arctic foxes were prime targets of the fur trade. Indigenous people made money from fox fur, using leg-hold traps and shooting as the primary hunting methods. Arctic foxes can sustain high hunting pressure due to their high reproductive capacity, but hunting during population lows could be harmful. Hunting has become much less common in recent decades, lowering the threat of overexploitation, but these animals are still subject to direct persecution in some areas.

Some populations have suffered from diseases spread from domestic dogs, including mange. Others face disease and persistent organic pollutants from the marine environment.

This species also has lost ground to the red fox. While arctic foxes are well adapted to cold and thick snow, the larger and more adaptable red foxes outcompete them in less extreme conditions. As climate change moves the snow line farther north, arctic foxes lose the camouflage advantage of their lighter coats. Scarcity of prey represents the biggest threat for the arctic fox, and mixing with foxes bred in captivity is also a threat.

This species and its dens gained legal protection in Sweden in 1928, in mainland Norway in 1930, and in Finland in 1940. In Europe, designation as a Priority species under the Actions by the Community relating to the Environment (ACE) provides full protection. In Svalbard,

Greenland, Canada, Russia, and Alaska, trapping is limited to licensed operators within a defined season.

How You Can Help

Symbolic adoption with Defenders of Wildlife supports the organization's efforts to pass legislation aimed at helping wildlife survive and adapt to climate change. Defenders also opposes opening up the Arctic Refuge to oil and gas development and works to educate the public about how climate change threatens arctic species, including the fox. There are four different levels of adoption support. Visit defenders.org; under Adopt an Animal, select the Arctic Fox.

Seeing Arctic Foxes in Scandinavia

Arctic foxes live throughout the Arctic. In Europe, visitors can see them on outings in Sweden and Norway.

Sweden

Sami Ecolodge near Ammarnäs village offers a four-day tour available June through August. Host and guide Mikael Vinka, a member of the indigenous Sami, works to help preserve these animals and brings a wealth of personal and inherited understanding of arctic flora and wildlife to his tours.

A nature reserve called Vindelfjällen, one of the largest protected areas in Europe, provides classic habitat for the arctic fox. The area contains a variety of alpine plants, and its mountains overlook the river delta. During the bright summer nights, guests may see arctic foxes carrying lemmings to their pups, as well as other wildlife such as golden eagles, elk, otter, and reindeer calves.

Tours include meals that focus on local food, with morning and evening meals served in front of the fireplace and lunches taken outdoors around an open fire. The food is made from Sami family recipes handed down through generations. Guests may choose between a traditional bed or sleeping on reindeer hides in a teepee. The lodge accommodates a maximum of 12 guests, so tours are small and intimate.

Norway

Lindblad Expeditions offers a trip, Land of the Ice Bears: An In-Depth Exploration of Arctic Svalbard, which takes groups in May and June to explore around the island of Svalbard on one of two well-appointed ships, *Orion* or *Explorer*. The tours travel from Oslo on a private charter flight to Longyearbyen, Svalbard, where the ships embark. Travel through the archipelago is exploratory by design, with exact day-to-day movements flexible and dependent on local conditions.

The main focus is searching for wildlife, including polar bears, reindeer, walruses, seals, and arctic foxes. The ships cruise Svalbard's fjords, and groups then travel by Zodiac and kayaks to explore the foot of glaciers, around icebergs, and along cliffs. "Pretty much every day we are off the ship and doing hikes or exploring in kayaks, although of course it is weather dependent," says Steve MacLean, who led Svalbard trips from 1988 through 2015.

The island of Svalbard does not have lemmings, so the foxes here feed around bird-breeding cliffs, taking eggs early in the season and chicks later on. "We fairly regularly see them there," MacLean says. "We watch them run around the bird cliffs, hunting, and sometimes see families just hanging out where the young pups are just playing." The foxes are no longer a beautiful white this time of year but already turning brown, which can make them hard to see on the cliffs. Sometimes, though, they are curious and come close, and the group gets a really good look, MacLean adds.

"The ships offer a wonderful combination of wilderness and comfort. You can be out watching foxes in the afternoon, and by evening, you have had a hot shower and are enjoying an adult beverage." Guests have a chance to explore Longyearbyen after the tour before the return flight to Oslo.

Travel Information

Lindblad Expeditions Land of the Ice Bears: An In-Depth Exploration of
Arctic Svalbard: (800) 397-3348, https://www.expeditions.com
/destinations/polar-regions/arctic/itineraries/land-of-the-ice-bears
-an-in-depth-exploration-of-arctic-svalbard/day-by-day/

Sami Ecolodge, Sweden: http://geunja.se

Travel tips The best time of year to visit is June through August in
Sweden; May for Svalbard, Norway. From early May to late August, it is
daylight almost around the clock in northern Scandinavia. Conversely,
in January and February, days are quite short. Winters are quite cold,
but summer temperatures are pleasant.

European bison herd in Knyszynska Forest, Poland
Credit: Piotr Wawrzyniak

European Bison

Bison bonasus

Poland

NATURETREK

Extinct in the wild by the late 1920s, the European bison now ranges free in protected areas in Poland, Lithuania, Belarus, Russian Federation, Ukraine, and Slovakia, thanks to reintroduction of captive animals from zoos. Europe's largest herbivore, it historically roamed throughout western, central, and southeastern Europe.

European bison, also known as wisent, live in deciduous and mixed forests and grassland habitats or meadow, including Poland's primeval Białowieża Forest. They look much like their North American relative, *B. bison*, with a thickset body, short neck, and pronounced shoulder hump, but slightly smaller. The European version also has a longer mane of hair underneath the neck and on the forehead, but its dark to golden-brown coat is not as shaggy. Both sexes of the European bison have short, upward-curving horns.

Adults are 9.5 feet long, stand up to a little more than 6 feet at the shoulder, and weigh as much as 2,200 pounds.

European and American bison share similar social systems, bachelor herds of males and maternal groups of 13 to 15 females, which include young with a dominant cow. Home ranges of these groups can include up to 38 square miles. Males join the female herds during mating season, August to October, and compete with each other for female attention. Gestation lasts about 264 days, and females typically give birth in May and July. Calves can run soon after birth and are weaned in about one year.

Bison eat grasses and browse on shoots and leaves. Adult males take in 70 pounds of food in a day during summer. The animals must drink every day and, during winter, break ice with their hooves to reach water. Though large, bison are quite agile, able to clear streams almost 10 feet wide or fences 6.5 feet high without a running start.

Threats to Bison

The IUCN Red List considers this species Vulnerable (www.iucnredlist.org/details/2814/0). It is not in-cluded in any CITES appendix. The global population of free-living European bison reached around 1,800 in 2006 and more than 4,000 by 2015.

Loss, degradation, and fragmentation of habitat due to agriculture and logging caused their extinction in the wild in the early nineteenth century. Unlimited hunting and poaching contributed as well. In Poland's Białowieża Forest, overpopulation of deer at the beginning of the nineteenth century caused drastic reduction of food for other herbivores, including bison. The conflicts of World War I and the Russian Revolution of 1917, combined with extensive poaching, further decimated the population.

Conflict and political instability continue to threaten reintroduced, free-living herds. Loss and fragmentation of habitat also remain serious threats. Contemporary Europe, especially in the west, contains little space for such a large herbivore, and human population density represents the most significant limiting factor to an increase in the number of European bison.

The current population descended from just 12 animals and is highly inbred. Inbreeding lowers resistance to disease and pathologies, and small, isolated populations of animals continue to lose genetic diversity. So far, conservationists have not found a way to facilitate migration of bison between herds.

Diseases represent a serious threat to the species, which may always have had low resistance or may have developed lowered immunity due to inbreeding. A disease that affects male reproductive organs was identified in the early 1980s in Białowieża Forest, but scientists have not yet determined its cause. Other diseases that threaten bison herds include foot-and-mouth disease and tuberculosis.

Hybridization or interbreeding with other species of bison poses a particular problem. Two free-living herds that contain hybrids of European and American bison live close to reintroduced, free-living pure European herds in the Caucasus. While the geography of mountain ridges and valleys make contact difficult if not impossible, the risk of these animals crossbreeding remains. Toksove Forest Park and the Mordovia Wildlife Reserve contain two small, semi-free herds of these hybrids as well.

Despite these continued threats, reintroduction of this species to the wild stands as an example of a conservation success story. Protection of European bison dates back to the fifteenth century through the eighteenth century, when people fed hay in winter to those living in the Białowieża. Reintroduction efforts began with establishment of the Bison Restitution Centre there in 1929 and, in 1948, of the Bison Breeding Centre in the Priokso-Terrasny Biosphere Reserve. The first captive-bred animals were released in 1952 in the Białowieża in Poland and, in 1953, on the Byelorussian side. Subsequently, bison have been reintroduced in Belarus, Poland, Russia, Lithuania, Slovakia, and Ukraine.

The Bison Specialist Group of the IUCN works using two different genetic lines to establish a total free-ranging population totaling about 6,000 animals. The European Bison Conservation Center (EBCC) involves breeders from Poland, Germany, Russia, Sweden, Spain, Romania, Belgium, Czech Republic, and Belarus in a coordinated program to preserve genetic variability within the captive population and to conduct reintroductions.

Seeing Bison in Poland

Naturetrek offers a four-day trip focusing on the birdlife of Poland's Białowieża Forest that also offers the chance to encounter European bison.

Tucked away on the easternmost fringes of Europe, the Białowieża Forest is the largest tract of untouched, primeval woodland on the continent and a UNESCO World Heritage Site. This vast patchwork of trees and wet meadows is one of Europe's most important wildlife habitats, home to a wide variety of species, including nine species of woodpeckers and elk or moose in addition to European bison. On bird-watching walks here and alongside the nearby Siemianówka Reservoir, tourists see red-breasted flycatcher, hazel grouse, nutcracker, barred warbler, white-winged black tern, and many others.

The tour goes to the Białowieża at dawn to search for woodpeckers, flycatchers, and other woodland species, says operations manager Paul Stanbury, and visits nearby wetlands for migrant waders, terns, waterfowl, and raptors, including lesser spotted eagle, white-tailed eagle, and Montagu's harrier. At dusk, the group looks for pygmy owls.

One morning is spent on a guided walk exploring the Strict Reserve, Białowieża's true primeval forest, which is largely untouched by humans. This trip is led by an expert Naturetrek ornithologist and a local naturalist guide. The group stays the night at a guesthouse in the village of Białowieża.

The outfitter also offers a seven-day Poland in Winter trip aimed at sighting large mammals rare or extinct in Western Europe, including European bison, wolf, and lynx. In winter, snow cover makes tracking these animals easier. The group explores the Puszcza Borecka forests, the most reliable site in Poland for sighting bison. To date, the tour has always seen them here. Other sightings typically include white-backed woodpecker, as well as roe deer, ravens, and white-tailed eagles.

Next the tour goes to northeastern Poland and the forests of Puszcza Romincka, Kaiser Wilhelm II's favorite hunting grounds, for four nights at Romincka. Here, experienced local foresters lead outings to see birds, mammals, and other winter wildlife and teach participants how to find mammals such as wolves by using tracks and signs. The group often travels by horse-drawn sleigh and may see wild boar, red fox, red and roe deer, elk, weasel, otter, European beaver, and, on rare occasions, even lynx. Optional nocturnal excursions offer the chance to see wolves from elevated blinds. Birds seen here include white-tailed eagle, sparrowhawk, goshawk, hazel grouse, black grouse, woodpecker, great gray shrike, hawfinch, crossbill, and nutcracker.

Because finding bison and other mammals proves so difficult in the Białowieża Forest in winter, this trip does not go there.

Travel Information

Naturetrek Poland's Primeval Forest: http://naturetrek.co.uk/tour
.aspx?id=357

Poland in Winter: http://naturetrek.co.uk/tour.aspx?id=360

Travel tips The best time of year to visit is May and January. Snow in winter makes animals easier to track and less wary of humans.

European mink
Credit: Nicolai Meyer

European Mink

Mustela lutreola

Danube Delta, Romania

VARIOUS OUTFITTERS

The European mink is a small carnivore once widespread on most of the continent but now remaining in only a few fragmented populations. The mink ranks among the most endangered mammals in Europe and in the world.

Medium-sized, mink have long, slender bodies, short legs, short bushy tails, and blackish-brown fur with a small band of white around their lips and, occasionally, on the throat. This marking helps distinguish the European mink from its larger cousin, the American mink (*M. vison*).

European mink inhabit densely vegetated banks of rivers, streams, and, sometimes during the warm season, the banks of lakes. These animals rarely stray more than about 100 yards from fresh water. Their dense, short coats have a thick, water-repellent undercoat that provides insulation when mink swim. Other adaptations for the semi-aquatic lifestyle include partly webbed feet for swimming, diving, and hunting underwater. Males and females look very much alike, although males are much larger than females. Young have an appearance similar to that of adults.

Mainly nocturnal, mink feed on insects and small animals, including water voles, birds, frogs, mollusks, crabs, and fish. They hunt both in the water and on land, relying primarily on smell to find their food.

The species occupies large home ranges of almost 10 miles of river. Females usually remain close to their dens, unless a shortage of food forces them to move farther. The animals live solitary lives except, of course, during breeding season in February and March. They use hisses, screams, and chuckling calls to find mates.

Gestation lasts 5 to 10 weeks, and young are born in spring when food and shelter are most available. Females have two to seven young per litter, which are born blind and helpless. Females raise the young alone in a den for five to six weeks, wean them at about 10 weeks, and they leave the den at 12 to 18 weeks. Mink have a life expectancy of about six years in the wild.

Threats to European Mink

This species appears as Critically Endangered on the IUCN Red List, and the IUCN Action Plan for Small Carnivores regards it as a Priority species for Europe and the world (www.iucnredlist.org/details/14018/0). It does not have any status under the ESA or CITES.

The European Union Habitats Directive lists this species in Annex II, meaning member states must designate special areas of conservation, and Annex IV, which requires a system for strict protection. The European mink is also protected by national law throughout its range (ec.europa .eu/environment/nature/legislation/habitatsdirective/index_en.htm).

In the past 10 years, it has lost more than half its population, a loss expected to intensify in the next 10 years due to habitat degradation and loss. Human activities have drastically altered the European continent, and resulting environmental change and disturbance have particularly affected the highly sensitive European mink.

The mink's range has decreased more than 85 percent since the midnineteenth century, currently consisting of only a few isolated fragments in northern Spain, western France, Romania's Danube delta, Ukraine, and Russia. The last wild mink in Estonia was caught in a trap in 1996. That country began efforts to establish a wild population in 2000, successfully creating a breeding population of approximately 100 individuals on Hiiumaa Island.

Other factors contributing to its precarious status include overexploitation for fur and introduction of American mink. A growing mink fur-farming industry in the former Soviet Union first introduced the alien American species, with some 24,000 released there prior to 1971. Plans for large-scale introductions in what is now Russia originally included only regions outside the European mink's natural range, but about 4,000 were released inside its range as well, as European mink became too scarce to sustain the fur-trapping industry. At the time, authorities did not view the American and European mink as two distinct species. A 2005 study in Denmark, a country with many mink farms, concluded that 86 percent of the American minks roaming free originally escaped from farms.

The effects of overhunting and habitat change further weakened European mink populations, increasing the negative effects of the spread of the American mink. Numerous records show American mink replacing European mink, but no reports of the reverse exist. While other causes of reduction in the European mink population can be controlled by conventional conservation management, little can be done to prevent spread of American mink. The presence of this invader across Europe complicates efforts to help the European mink recover. An additional complication comes from the popularity of American minks as pets in France.

Other threats include hybridization, road casualties, Aleutian disease, and unintentional trapping and poisoning as part of efforts to control various pests.

Reintroducing Mink in Estonia

The Lutreola Foundation, a species conservation organization started in 1992, has focused on conservation of the European mink and efforts to restore populations on the Estonian islands of Hiiumaa and Saaremaa. The foundation's stated goals include preservation of biological diversity; research, management, and policies on biodiversity; public awareness of use and conservation of species; and performance of respective species conservation projects.

Lutreola works with the Tallinn Zoological Gardens. After mink disappeared from the wild in Estonia in 1996, the zoo established a captive population to help prevent extinction of the species. The first of its European mink were introduced back into the Estonian wild in 2001. Visitors can see the breeding population of about 100 minks in its new facility at the zoo.

Seeing Mink in Romania

The Danube originates in the German Black Forest and flows a distance of 1,777 miles across 10 countries to the delta, where it flows into the Black Sea. Floating islands on the delta are home to otters, stoats, wild cats, and European mink.

The size of the area's mink population is unknown and seeing them is difficult, but it does happen. People visit the delta's network of channels, lakes, and forests—one of the last natural places in Europe—for the chance to see more than 300 migratory and resident bird species, including eagles, egrets, vultures, geese, cranes, ibises, cormorants, swans, and pelicans. The entire Danube delta became a Biosphere Reserve in 1990.

Ibis Tours offers trips aboard a floating hotel on the Danube, beginning at Tulcea on the Black Sea. It travels to the Lagoon of Sahalin Peninsula, one of the most important spots for bird migration and breeding in the Danube delta. Flocks of white and Dalmatian pelicans fishing the waters of this lagoon sometimes come very close to the boat. The floating hotel travels on the Sulina arm and moors on a remote part of the Old Danube for the first night.

The route then follows the Channel of Magearu to Letea Village and explores Lakes Trei Iezere, Matita, and Furtuna. Large flocks of fishing pelicans also frequent these areas.

Outfitter Tioc Natur und Studienreisen offers trips in the Danube delta as well, starting in Tulcea and traveling on an eight-room pontoon boat. For five days, the group explores via small motorboats, which allow access into smaller channels for better observation of wildlife, including the possibility of spotting mink. Tours often see birds such as cormorant, glossy ibis, white and Dalmatian pelican, and red-footed falcon. The trip wraps up with a visit to a World Wildlife Fund coordinated project in Letea forest and village.

Eco Chettusia has trips of from 4 to 10 days, starting in Tulcea and traveling by boat, staying in guesthouses and hotels on land each night. Guides speak English, French, and Italian, and Spanish- or German-speaking guides are available on request. Participants see 120 to 150 species of birds in spring and summer and the chance to spot mink.

Travel Information

Tallinn Zoological Gardens: http://tallinnzoo.ee/en/animal/european-mink/

Ibis Tours: http://ibis-tours.ro/danube-delta-tour.php

Tioc Natur: http://tioc-reisen.ro/index.php?tour=2

Eco Chettusia: http://chettusia.com/tours

Travel tips The best time of year to visit is April through September. Water levels are high in spring, meaning more travel by boat and less on land. Check the CDC website for the latest status of measles outbreaks.

Iberian lynx in Spain
Credit: Program Ex-situ Conservation

Iberian Lynx

Lynx pardinus

Spain

VARIOUS OUTFITTERS

The Iberian lynx, a beautiful cat, has a tawny coat with dark spots, beard-like fur around its face, prominent black ear tufts, and a black tip on its short tail. Adults weigh 22 to 28 pounds and stand about 3 feet tall.

Generally nocturnal, they become most active at twilight when hunting. Both sexes are solitary and territorial, with male territories overlapping those of several females. Mating season is from December to February, and females generally give birth between March and April. Gestation lasts 60 to 70 days, and average litter size is three, with two typically surviving. Most females make their dens at the base of old, hollow cork oak trees.

After 20 days, the mother moves her kittens to as many as three or four other dens, perhaps to give them more room and help protect them against discovery by predators. The young eat solid food by 28 days but nurse for up to four months, leaving the den around 10 months of age.

Independent young females may remain in their mother's territory for up to 20 months or more. Males and females usually acquire their own territory before breeding, which may require waiting until another lynx dies or moves on. Females with their own territory are able to breed at two years of age. These animals may live up to 13 years in the wild.

Iberian lynx eat mostly wild rabbits, but when rabbits become scarce, lynx also hunt ducks, young deer, and partridges. Adults eat about one rabbit a day, but a mother with young needs three or more.

Threats to Iberian Lynx

The Iberian lynx ranks as the world's most threatened species of cat. The species appears as Endangered on the IUCN Red List, after spending more than 10 years as Critically Endangered, and in CITES Appendix I (www.iucnredlist.org/details/12520/0).

In the early nineteenth century, the Iberian lynx roamed throughout Spain, Portugal, and southern France. Its population and range declined steadily during the twentieth century, and by 2000 only two isolated breeding populations in southern Spain remained. In 2012, the population totaled 156 adult animals. This improvement in status, due to intensive and ongoing conservation efforts, resulted in the change from Critically Endangered to Endangered.

Future increase in range and population may require additional reintroductions; without them, extinction is possible within 30 years or so. A major future threat includes decrease in availability of prey. Rabbits have been affected by epidemics, including hemorrhagic disease, and authorities may need to escalate efforts to recover rabbit populations.

High-speed roads and highways split the lynx habitat, and vehicles represent another major threat to these cats—just as they do to endangered panthers in Florida and ocelots in Texas. In 2014, for example, 22 lynx were killed by cars, a significant number given their small population. Another threat comes from habitat loss and degradation as a result of infrastructure such as roads, dams, and railways and other human activities. Between 1960 and 1990, as much as 80 percent of the range of this species may have been lost. Loss of cork trees in particular affects reproduction success.

Illegal hunting remains a threat; people kill the cats for their fur and meat and also because some consider them a threat to populations of game animals. The species has enjoyed legal protection from hunting since the early 1970s, but people still shoot and trap them, and they are caught in traps and snares set for other animals.

How You Can Help

Drink wine! Wine, that is, that comes in a bottle sealed with a real cork. Cork bark can be harvested from trees once they reach about 25 years of age and every 10 years after. The trees live as long as 250 years, and each produces enough cork to stopper 4,000 wine bottles. The ancient Greeks were the first to use cork as stoppers, mainly for olive and wine jars.

Cork represents an environmentally and economically sustainable industry, as the bark grows back after harvest. Forests of these trees also help maintain watersheds, prevent erosion, and keep soils healthy. As long as people residing in the area can make a living from cork, they will protect these valuable trees, which provide habitat for numerous endemic species, some of them rare. If people cannot make a living from cork, they may convert the cork forest to less sustainable uses.

Increasing use of alternative stoppers, including plastic corks and screw-off caps, threatens the cork industry—and, therefore, western Mediterranean ecosystems. Loss of the industry would mean increased poverty and decreased biodiversity. Choose wine with cork stoppers by looking for the Forest Stewardship Council (FSC) certification on wine labels, or simply buy a wine that you already know has a real cork stopper.

Seeing Lynx in Spain

Three outfitters arrange trips through natural areas in Spain to see many kinds of wildlife, including, for lucky travelers, Iberian lynx.

Naturetrek Holiday

Naturetrek offers a six-day holiday to the Coto Doñana National Park and Sierra Morena, home to a wealth of mammals and birds in addition to Iberian lynx. Two nights are spent at El Rocío, a village overlooking the park's lagoon, river, and marshlands, one of Europe's prime wetlands. The group heads out in four-wheel-drive vehicles before dawn and again in the afternoon, bumping through the mosaic of old woodland, reed beds, and freshwater and saline lagoons and settling in place for spotting lynx as they become active. A Naturetrek naturalist and expert local guide accompany each excursion, and four out of five tours see lynx.

"We are rewarded with a sighting for about every twelve hours we spend in the habitat," says general manager Andy Tucker. "They are not easy to see, and the quality of sightings depends somewhat on luck. We have had them trot right out in front of us or seen them asleep in the grass where you can't get good photographs." Roughly 30 percent of the remaining lynx population lives in this area.

The outings also present an opportunity to see red and fallow deer, hares and rabbits, wild boar, and otter, along with birds of prey and migrants such as storks, herons, waders, ducks, gulls, and terns. The region's birds also include purple gallinule, marbled teal, crested coot, the rare Spanish imperial eagle, and red-necked nightjar.

Next the tour goes to the hills of Sierra Morena, northeast of Seville, for three nights. This is very different habitat, and the group stations at spots with panoramic views of the mixed grassland and pine landscape. "We use binoculars and scopes, scanning vast tracts of lynx habitat from high viewpoints, to look for movement, particularly at dawn and dusk," Tucker says. While doing so, the group enjoys tremendous scenery, wildlife such as deer and otter, and birdlife including azure-winged magpies and hawfinches.

Groups are limited to 13 people. Naturetrek's sustainable tourism policy states that the company is run by naturalists with acute interests in conservation and the need to ensure the long-term protection of species and habitats. "We stay in local hotels, eat at local restaurants, and employ local guides to take us into the park," Tucker adds. "Locals are very aware of the economic benefit of bird-watchers and wildlife watchers in Doñana, and we are acutely aware that the animals need to be valuable to the locals in order to be protected. The best way we can assist these animals is by bringing people to see them and contribute to the local economy."

Iberian Lynx Tour with Birdwatching Spain

This outfitter's Iberian lynx tour focuses on Andújar in Jaén province. It includes a stop at the Laguna de Fuente la Piedra to see flamingos, common cranes, hen and black-winged kites, waders, and other wildfowl before continuing to the heart of Sierra de Andújar. The next two days include visits to the best viewing points to watch wildlife, including wild boar, red and fallow deer, mouflon sheep, Spanish ibex, and otter in addition to lynx.

Participants also see abundant raptors—golden eagle, black and griffon vulture, and Spanish imperial eagle—as well as azure-winged magpie, hoopoe, blue rock thrush, Iberian green woodpecker, and Sardinian and Dartford warblers in the Mediterranean forest.

Before flying out of Spain, travelers spend time in the Guadalhorce River watching Cetti's warblers, penduline tits, reed buntings, white-headed ducks, common teals, shovelers, Audouin's gulls, and other wildfowl.

Pau Lucio, who has guided these trips since 2010, says, "It is a very exciting and rewarding experience. You have to be patient, but while we wait for lynx to show up, there is lots of other wildlife to see. We spend most of the time watching from viewing spots. However, we take short strolls every day to see other wildlife, mainly birds. Sometimes we are lucky enough to see lynx just a few meters away, and once we watched a male and female for more than two hours. I would say that the chance of seeing one is around ninety percent on my five-day trips in early winter, which is the mating season when they are very active. On a shorter trip and in other seasons, chances are lower."

Julian Sykes Wildlife Holidays Lynx Tour

This tour also explores the Sierra Morena, specifically the Sierra de Andújar in northern Andalucía, where most of the world population of Iberian lynx lives. This last remaining pristine Mediterranean forest of cork oak and other trees, rivers, glades, and meadows is also home to otter, wild boar, mouflon, deer, and raptors such as Spanish imperial and golden eagles.

The tour spends three days in Sierra de Andújar Natural Park, in rooms whose balconies or terraces overlook woods and mountains. Azure-winged magpie, short-toed treecreeper, firecrest, nuthatch, and other birds live on the grounds. Early morning and late afternoon each day, the group searches for lynx from strategic points, spending the rest of the day walking, driving within the reserve, and relaxing at the hotel complex.

"I have now made more than seventy visits to the lynx site, usually for the standard four-night stay, which allows for eight realistic chances of seeing an animal," says Sykes. "Currently, I'm running at a hit rate of around ninety-five percent, which is pretty good. The times I miss tend to be away from the winter months, when the cats are less active during the day."

Sightings occur both from very short observations at close range to watching the cats for more than an hour at a distance of about 300 yards. The group may see more than one individual, and sometimes, females moving around with their offspring.

"Seeing the world's rarest cat is simply superb, and added to that, it is a gorgeous animal that commands a respect from the land it occupies," Sykes says. "They are just awesome."

Travel Information

Naturetrek Holiday, Spain: http://naturetrek.co.uk/tour.aspx?id=98

Birdwatching Spain: http://birdwatchingspain.net/iberian-lynx-tour/

Julian Sykes Wildlife Holidays, Spain: http://juliansykeswildlife.com/
IberianLynxinAndalucia.html

Travel tips The best time of year to visit is October through January. Expect cool temperatures with rain and fog possible.

Index